Indoor Plants

Indoor Plants

Contents

First published 1975 by
Octopus Books Limited
59 Grosvenor Street, London W.1.

© 1975 Octopus Books Limited

ISBN 0 7064 0476 9

Produced by Mandarin Publishers Limited
Westlands Road, Quarry Bay, Hong Kong
Printed in Hong Kong

Introduction

Growing indoor or house plants has always been popular. For generations, cottage windows have been traditionally brightened by colourful displays, while a century ago, no 'parlour' was complete without a dusty Aspidistra lurking in the comparative gloom of its surroundings. But never has the cultivation of house plants been more popular than today, when trends towards open plan houses and offices, large picture windows and lighter, brighter, living conditions, have considerably extended the range of plants that can be grown indoors.

House plants have an important role to play in the practical and economic necessities of modern life. It is true that in principle they fulfil the same job as cut flowers, but not only do they demand less attention to keep them looking at their best, they quite clearly last considerably longer. Apart from invigorating indoor life with their freshness, they can be used as room dividers, as screens to hide less attractive areas or as focal points in their own right. They can be grown singly in pots or bowls, together in dish gardens or troughs, trailing from hanging baskets or contained in bottles.

In this book we have attempted to describe several of the most commonly known and grown indoor plants, and some of the more unusual ones, along with the conditions of light, warmth and watering they need to flourish. In addition there are some hints on plant selection and propagation, making dish and bottle gardens and some suggestions for various ways of 'using' plants.

(below) A colourful
display of flowering and
foliage indoor plants
(right) Foliage indoor
plants growing in a dish
garden

Plant Selection and Care

Nowadays there are an amazing number and variety of plants cultivated to be grown indoors. The growing requirements and care that they need as individuals are almost as varied, and undoubtedly make it essential to consider the conditions under which your plants will be expected to flourish, before becoming too ambitious in your choice. Personal preferences for plants with lovely foliage or for those that produce beautiful flowers, must be considered alongside other factors.

The three main points to take into account before bringing plants into your home are: firstly, general aspects of the growing situation – how much light is there in the room where the plants will be kept? Is it permanently heated in some way, or are there periods when it is very cold? Is the plant required for a spot that is always cool and shady or for a place that attracts lots of sun?

Secondly, consider the purpose for which the plants are wanted. Are they to offset a table or desk, or to act as a room divider or screen? Should they compliment the decor of the room or blend in with the view from a window?

Thirdly, some relevant points about the owner-to-be. Is he, or she, an experienced 'indoor gardener' with a wealth of hard-earned knowledge and experience; or a beginner who knows little about plant care? Above all, how much time do they have to devote to looking after indoor plants?

The answers to these questions, coupled with some knowledge of the different requirements of individual plants – which we discuss in the following chapters of this book – will help you to decide which indoor plants would make the most suitable choice. If you are a beginner, start with some of the 'easy-to-grow' plants that need minimal attention, and progress to the more demanding as you become more experienced.

Although, as we have said, plants have individual requirements, there are several aspects of plant care that can be applied generally to house plants. They all need, light, for example, in order to grow at all, although the extent varies.

In general, plants will flourish best if they are kept in the lightest place in a room. This is likely to be as near to the window as possible. Keep them out of direct sunlight though, which damages most plants. It will help if you keep curtains and blinds fully open for as long as possible during the day. It is reasonable to assume in such conditions, however, that the main light source will be coming from one direction only, and as plants tend to grow towards the light, turn them slightly each week so that all parts are exposed to the maximum light source in turn. This ensures that they grow symmetrically and not considerably faster on one side. It should be done whether the plant is kept on the window sill, or in the centre of the room.

If there is insufficient light in the room, the best method of artificial lighting is fluorescent, as ordinary light bulbs or reflector floods create too much heat. Such heat is even more acute when bulbs are used in the enclosed areas in the strengths necessary to produce the required illumination. Strangely enough, contrary to any feeling that plants will grow better in natural light, they are equally as happy with good artificial light. Plants lit artificially, however, should be checked frequently for danger signals. For example, if a plant lit by fluorescent light begins to turn yellow, it is receiving too much light. It should be moved away from the light source or exposed for a shorter period of time each day.

The demands of house plants for warmth are even more variable than those for light, because of the immensely different climatic conditions found in their natural habitats. The biggest menace to any plant, however, is fluctuations of temperature. Long periods in the day when rooms are not heated to a great extent, followed by a period in the evening, perhaps, when the room becomes quickly overheated, followed once more by a rapid fall in the temperature during the night, makes life very difficult for plants!

Central heating has undoubtedly contributed greatly in making houses suitable places for growing plants as it helps to maintain more constant temperatures. Next to central heating, the best way to heat a room is with a slow-burning solid fuel stove that is alight all night. Paraffin oil burners and gas fires are less advisable as many plants are adversely affected by their fumes.

Try to keep plants in places in the room where the temperature is as uniform as possible. Avoid standing them on a mantel-

piece above a fireplace or a shelf over a radiator, where they are likely to be roasted for part of the day and then considerably cooled when the heat is turned down or switched off. Behind the curtains on a window sill at night is another bad place, as it is likely to be intensely cold, if not freezing, in winter-time.

As a general rule, the ideal continuous day temperature is 60°–70°F (15°–21°C), with a minimum of 45°F (7°C) at night. In the following chapters of this book, you will find individual temperature requirements given for many plants. Some people recommend a lower constant winter temperature, at which point the plant will survive, but not grow. This is because the growth made during the short daylight hours of winter is usually not very decorative. The stems are liable to become spindly and drawn and the leaves, small and discoloured. Foliage plants are particularly prone to this, and in the spring you should nip out all growing points and bad growth made in the winter, so that the new growth will be healthy and bushy.

Fresh air is important to indoor plants too. They appreciate being stood outside for a time on mild days, or put in a room on a warm day with the windows wide open. Make sure however, that they are not standing in draughts.

A great many house plants are evergreens that grow naturally in tropical countries, and therefore flourish best in humid conditions. As humidity indoors is disagreeable to people, it can be created specifically for plants. There are two successful ways of doing this – one is to keep the potted plant standing in another large pot, and the space between them packed with peat, which must be kept continuously moist.

The other way is to put some small pebbles in a container, pour water over to nearly cover the pebbles and stand the potted plant on top. (The base of the pot must be kept free from the water.)

Water, and how much a plant needs, is another basic essential about which it is hard to generalise. It varies so much, according to the characteristics of individual plants, the season of the year and the conditions in which they are kept. Plants with fleshy leaves such as cacti and succulents, can retain water within their tissues, and thus require less frequent watering than others. Plants with proportionately large and broad leaves require frequent watering as they have a larger leaf surface from which they 'breathe' out water vapour. Plants kept in cool places need less water than those in warm, bright places and plants in well-drained pots, porous clay pots or small pots generally need more watering than those in larger or plastic pots.

All these points have to be considered individually, but general rules would be to water fairly frequently during the plant's growing season, which is usually in the spring and summer, and to give considerably less in its resting period. Each watering should be thorough, perhaps every seven to ten days. Daily dribbles are useless. If possible, use water that has had the chill taken off, and water in the morning during winter. Most important of all – it is better to under-water than over-water.

Probably the best way to give water, and essential for plants such as cyclamen, is to plunge the pots to half their depth in a bowl of water. Leave them like this until their soil is moist, but not so long it becomes water-logged, drain the pots and replace them in their usual position.

Plants can also be watered from above, in which case there should be a space of about one inch between the rim and the soil. A small watering can with a long, narrow spout is the best sort, as it allows you to water the plant without wetting its leaves. With the exception of a few water-loving plants, such as *Helxine soleirolii*, house plants should never stand permanently in a dish of water. The methods mentioned to provide humidity, can also be a help when the demand for water is very high, if watering can only be carried out infrequently, or if the owner is away for a day or two.

Most indoor plants benefit from occasional doses of one of the proprietary feeds available on the market. Such feeds should be given when the soil is moist, and only during the plant's growing season. Give in the quantities recommended by the manufacturers.

An aspect of plant care that is perhaps sometimes overlooked, is that of sponging the leaves. Plants 'breathe' through their leaves, and indoors, where they are not washed naturally by rain, they tend to get clogged by dust and grime. To relieve this, sponge the leaves regularly on both upper and lower surfaces, using a piece of cotton wool and luke-warm water. Treat mature leaves only in this way – delicate foliage should be sprayed instead.

As plants grow, so inevitably do their roots, and it will eventually become necessary to re-pot them. Most house plants, however, flourish best in what would appear to be too small a pot, so don't be in too much of a hurry to re-pot.

Signs that indicate a plant needs repotting, are a slowing up of growth, rapid drying out of soil and the roots growing through the drainage hole. A final test is to gently tip the plant out of its pot and if there is a mass of matted roots with barely any soil visible, the plant is 'pot-bound' and needs re-potting. A pot one size larger will be adequate – use two sizes larger, only if the plant grows very vigorously.

If you are using a clay pot, put a layer of crocks over the drainage hole, then a thin layer of peat and a layer of potting compost. Gently loosen a few of the matted outside roots, disturbing the root ball as little as possible, and put it on top of the compost. Fill in the space between it and the pot with moist compost up to the base of the plant's stem (which should be about one-inch below the rim of the pot). Press down the compost so there is no gap between the old and new soil ball. Water the plant well straight away and put it in a shady place for a week. This re-potting procedure can also be followed when potting-up new plants.

Plants generally need re-potting annually for the first few years. The usual progression is from a three-inch pot to a five-inch one and then to a six-inch. At this point, it usually suffices to re-pot every other year. Most house plants are unlikely to grow too large for an eight-inch pot, and as they are rather difficult to re-pot anyway, they should be 'top-dressed' instead. This entails removing the top two inches of soil each spring and replacing it with fresh compost enriched by extra fertilizer.

Re-pot when the plant is in full growth. May is the best month for most house plants, and a good compost to use is a mixture of two parts commercial potting compost and one part garden peat. The soilless composts you can buy are also good.

Indoor plants will put out 'distress signals' as things go wrong and if you catch and treat these in time, the plants may still have some chance of survival. Some common points are discussed below.

Slow growth in summer means the plant is being over-watered or under-fed. In winter, slow growth merely means the plant is resting.

If the plant begins to wilt, it could mean that it needs watering, but, beware, because it could also mean that it has already been over-watered. Check to see if the soil ball is very dry or over saturated. If it is dry, the plant will probably recover when it has been well watered. If it has been over-watered, it is not so easy to save. The only hope for recovery is to place the plant in a warm place immediately and water it very

moderately until it has recovered.

Too sunny or hot a position also makes plants wilt, but they will usually recover if removed to somewhere cooler and shadier, and lightly sprayed with cool water.

Yellowing leaves and straggly growth are signs that the plant has been over-watered, is in too warm a place if it is summer-time, or that it needs re-potting. If the leaves begin to fall after turning yellow, it could be because the plant is in a draught, it has insufficient humidity or the temperature is too low. It could also indicate that it is being overcome by gas fumes or an attack of red spider mites. You can detect the latter by the presence of a fine whitish, silken web on the underside of the leaves, where the mites live, and eliminate them by spraying with petroleum white oil emulsion.

If spots appear on the foliage and the tips of the leaves go brown, it could again be a sign of over-watering, over-heating, low humidity or that the plant has been subjected to draughts. This could also happen, however, because the plant has been given too much fertilizer or that it has been scorched by splashing during watering. You should be able to detect or deduce the cause and act accordingly.

If the soil surrounding the plant is very wet and the plant's leaves are beginning to droop, it almost inevitably means that the plant has been over-watered and its roots are rotting as a result. Treat as previously described for over-watering, but don't be too optimistic that the plant will recover.

If the leaves of a variegated plant begin to

come through green all over, it is an indication of insufficient light reaching it.

Besides red spider mites already mentioned, there are other pests which attack indoor plants. Happily these occur fairly infrequently, particularly if the plants are regularly inspected and leaves are cleaned as previously described. Among the more common pests are:

Greenfly or **Aphids**. These are sap suckers, which cover the leaves and stems of plants, with a sticky substance and eventually distort them. The odd few can be picked off, but if there are many, they should be sprayed with malathion or a systemic insecticide.

White Flies. Also sapsuckers, these make the plant's foliage mottled. Spray with malathion.

Scale insects. You can detect the presence of these if the stems and underside of leaves are covered with off-white scales interspersed with mobile orange scales – the young insects. Remove them with cotton wool soaked in methylated spirits and mounted on the end of a thin stick.

Mealy Bugs. Look like tufts of cotton, these are sap feeders which will stunt and distort the plant's growth. Treat in the same way as Scale insects.

The most common diseases to affect indoor plants are mildew and rot. In the former, the leaves become distorted and covered with a white powder. Remove affected parts whenever possible and spray the plant with Karathane.

Rot is caused by overwatering or allowing water to remain on leaves, stems and growing centres. Again, cut the affected parts away if possible and thereafter keep it fairly warm, while watering it very sparingly. If it recovers, take care in the future not to allow water to remain on the plant.

Many houseplants can be propagated and there are a variety of ways of doing this. As so many indoor plants become unruly and ill-shaped after a few years, propagation is an ideal way of replacing them.

Plants such as *Chlorophytum*, *Ficus pumila*, *Ficur radicans* and *Saxifraga sarmentosa*, which all send out runners with tufts of leaves growing at their tips, can be propagated by 'layering'. To do this make a slanting incision in the stem in the vicinity of this growth, remove the leaves and peg down the growing point securely in potting compost in another pot. Leave it like this for about five weeks, during which time roots will form and grow down into the soil. After this period, cut the plantlet off from its parent, and re-pot if necessary. (The plants mentioned above and subsequently will be described and discussed in later chapters in this book.)

Plants which lose their lower leaves as they mature, such as *Ficus elastica*, *Cordyline terminalis*, *Fatshedera lizei* and various types of dracaena and dieffenbachia can be replaced by 'air-layering'. Cut a narrow ring in the bark at a point about twelve inches below the tip of the plant. Moisten this with water and apply hormone rooting compound to it with a camel-hair brush. Cover it with a generous handful of sphag-

num moss, bound in position with raffia and then cover it completely with a small sheet of polythene. Fix this to the stem with cellophane tape. When you can see the new roots through the polythene, cut the stem below the bundle of moss, remove the new plant and pot it in the usual way. You can in fact, resuscitate the old plant by cutting the remaining stem down to soil level, water and feed it and new shoots will soon appear.

Many indoor houseplants can be propagated by cuttings. There are three types of cutting – stem, heel and leaf.

Plants that respond to stem cuttings include the ivies, *Rhoicissus rhomboidea*, *Cissus antarctica* and some philodendrons. To propagate in this way, cut a shoot just below a leaf joint, i.e. about six inches from its tip, using a sharp knife or razor blade. Remove all buds and leaves from the lower half.

Heel cuttings are usually taken from wooded plants. Tear a shoot off the older stem leaving a 'heel' or bark. Reduce this to about six inches long and remove all buds and leaves from its lower half.

Leaf cuttings are particularly suitable for saintpaulias and begonias. Cut off an adult leaf at its point of origin using a razor blade or sharp knife. Make sure it has a sizeable length of stem.

All cuttings should be planted to a depth of at least half an inch in a potting medium, such as a commercial potting compost or a soil-less compost. (In the case of leaf cuttings, the stalk is inserted to this length or deeper in the compost.) When planted, water them and cover the pots with clear polythene bags or invert large glass jam jars over them to provide a humid atmosphere. Ideally, you should stand the pots on a warm window-sill or above a radiator.

The best time to take cuttings is between mid-May and mid-August and the worst time is during the winter, when rooting will probably not take place at all. Rooting usually takes place sometime between 3 and 6 weeks after taking the cutting, and new leaves are a fairly reliable sign the cutting has been successful. Alternatively, give it a gentle tug and if it gives some resistance it has probably taken. If it comes out, merely re-insert it in the compost and leave it for a longer period.

When the cuttings have rooted, remove the polythene bags or jars and leave the cuttings in their pots for a week or so. Then re-pot them, taking care not to damage the roots which are very delicate at this stage. Leave in a warm place for another week, before moving them to their permanent growing position.

Another means of propagating is by 'division', and is a suitable method for plants such as *Aspidistra lurida* and *Spathiphyllum wallisii*, which produce small 'offsets' round the parent plants. These consist of a few leaves with roots attached and may be detached and potted up in the usual way.

Plants for Foliage

Houseplants grown for their beautiful foliage form the largest group of indoor plants and many of them are very easy to maintain. There would appear to be a foliage house plant to suit every situation as there are types that grow in a 'bushy or upright' way, while others climb and trail. In addition we will also be discussing ferns and palms in this chapter as strictly speaking these are grown for their foliage. They are, perhaps often associated with bygone days, conjuring up thoughts of 'front parlours' and pre-war seaside hotels, but they have an elegance that is equally at home in contemporary and modern decor.

Bushy and Upright Foliage Plants
Begonia rex. This beautiful plant, which is a great favourite, is one of the few species of the prolific Begonia group which is grown exclusively for its foliage. (Other varieties will be discussed in Plants for Flowers.) The colour of its large, almost triangular leaves covers a wide range – from silver to dark green and pink to the deepest purple. The beautiful patterns on the leaves are composed of dots, stripes and splashes of numerous contrasting colours with bands on their edges and along the path of their veins.

It should be kept in semi-shade, out of reach of gas fumes and grows best if kept in an outer container filled with moist peat (see page 12). Water it well during the summer, less ·in winter and take care not to splash the leaves at any time. It likes a winter temperature that remains fairly constant at about 50°–55°F., (10°–13°C).

Cordyline terminalis has large tapering leaves which are pink, cerise or cream when young and eventually become mainly green and red with splashings and margins of brighter colour. It rarely exceeds two-feet in height and should be grown in rich soil, containing a good amount of peat or leaf-mould. It likes an average to light room and fairly frequent watering in the summer.

Popular names for Cordylines are the Flaming Dragon Tree or the Scarlet Aspidistra.

Pilea cadierei. There are various species of pilea, most of which are very decorative, small, bushy plants. Pileas are generally quick and easy to grow, favouring an average to warm room. They are excellent components for a bottle garden or as a low feature of a dish garden. Most pileas dislike strong sunshine, and during the summer, they like plenty of water and feeds of liquid manure.

Pilea cadierei is popularly known as the Aluminium or Friendship Plant. It has pointed oval leaves that are dark green with broken aluminium stripes. There is also a dwarf version called *Pilea cadierei* 'Nani'.

Pilea muscosa, known also as the Artillery Gunpowder or Pistol Plant is unlike *Pilea cadierei* to look at, but likes similar conditions in which to grow. It has tiny, light-green, moss-like foliage and is quite often used in hanging baskets.

Aspidistra lurida, known as the Cast Iron or Parlour Plant, is one of the most famous and hardiest of all foliage house plants. It is prepared to withstand gas fumes, deep shade, neglect, heat, dust, dryness of air and soil – almost anything apparently adverse, except bright sunlight! Ideally it likes a reasonable supply of moisture, medium humidity and fair warmth.

The beautiful large, upright leaves may be dark green or variegated, and both are much prized by flower arrangers for their spectacular display. Unfortunately aspidistras are becoming something of a rarity nowadays. They are slow growers and tend to be rather costly to purchase.

If you do acquire one, sponge its leaves occasionally and stand it out of doors for a while in warm summer rain.

Sansevieria trifasciata 'Laurentii' has lovely narrow, fleshy, pointed and slightly twisted leaves edged with yellow and banded alternately with light and dark green. It grows straight up to a height of about two-feet or more. Commonly known as Mother-in-Law's Tongue or the Bayonet or Snake Plant, it is easy to grow, liking sunshine, but happy also to grow in shadier conditions. Water it weekly in summer and monthly in winter, letting it dry out between waterings.

Helxine soleirolii. This little plant is very easy to grow, but as it tends to be rather evasive, it should be used carefully.

It has bright green, rounded foliage and is unusual in that it likes to stand permanently in a saucer of water. Be sure not to wet the foliage, however, particularly in winter when it is liable to rot.

Its ideal growing situation is a moist,

cool, partially shady place away from gas fumes. Popularly known as Mind Your Own Business, Baby's Tears and Irish or Japanese Moss, it can be successfully used to carpet the soil beneath a single plant or a group of plants.

Ficus elastica 'Decora'. This is one of the popular 'Rubber Plants', and of all the house plants belonging to the ficus genera, it is probably the best known. It is fair to say that it has almost taken the place of the Victorian Aspidistra in modern living.

It is a good looking plant that will eventually grow to eight-feet or more and certainly imparts drama to the decor of many modern rooms. (You can keep it smaller by cutting it back in the spring while it is growing!) It has large, dark-green, shiny leaves, that emerge from a bright red sheath, looking almost like a flower.

Keep it out of direct sunlight and draughts and water it generously in the summer, at which time it also appreciates feeds of liquid manure. Wash its leaves frequently in luke-warm water and keep it in a smallish pot for its size. It is a hardy plant and able to adapt to varying temperatures.

Ficus benjamina is more difficult to cultivate than other species of ficus, but by no means impossible. It needs a well lit warm room in which the temperature never falls below 50°F (10°C), but it should be kept out of direct sunlight. Beware of over-watering particularly in the winter. Keep it moist during the summer but let it dry out almost completely between waterings. If it be-comes too dry, however, it tends to wilt.

Ficus benjamina is a graceful house plant with ovate leaves that terminate abruptly in a sharp point. If it is allowed to, it will grow to a tall, weeping tree. Its popular names are the Weeping or Willow Fig.

Ficus pandurata or *Ficus lyrata* is another member of this genera and is superb for spacious premises such as offices or a large entrance hall. It has strikingly shaped leaves, that somewhat resemble a violin in shape and are beautifully marked with cream coloured veins. They eventually grow to a length of eighteen inches.

Ficus pandurata is a little more difficult to grow than *Ficus elastica* 'Decora', but the conditions it needs are much the same. *Fittonia argyroneura*, pictured on page 21, is a low growing plant that is rather difficult to grow because of its demand for warmth and humidity coupled with an inability to stand great heat. It grows best in a bottle garden, but if you grow it elsewhere, keep it away from draughts and in an outer container filled with damp peat. Over-watering and allowing it to get too dry are equally damaging.

As you can see from the illustration, it is an attractive plant with roundish dark green leaves, heavily veined with silver.

Dracaena or Dragon Plant. There are many varieties of Dracaena, all of which are very lovely, comparatively tall and slow growing plants. Some of them are often confused with *Cordyline terminalis* (see page 20).

Most varieties have long, firm, silky,

pointed leaves that are variously striped, and which tend to be shed as the plant grows taller. Most Dracaena will grow happily in average home conditions, although they need a temperature that is never lower than 55°F (13°C). They also like some humidity. Water them freely in the summer – considerably less in the winter. They are happy in bright and medium light, but keep variegated types out of direct sunlight.

Two dwarf species which make attractive house plants are the *Dracaena godseffiana* which has dark-green leaves with pale yellow spots, and the *Dracaena sanderi* or *sanderiana*, known also as the Variegated Dragon Tree. It has lance-shaped, grey green leaves that have a white border. It is a rather delicate plant flourishing only in a warm temperature with moist air and semi-shade – requirements that make it a good component for a bottle garden.

Fatsia japonica. Popularly called Aralia, Fig Leaf Palm and the Castor Oil Plant, this is a hardy house plant which is able to flourish in shady spots out of doors when the weather is warm. As an indoor plant it grows easily and can become quite large. This makes it useful for dramatic display in a large area, but it can be kept bushy by topping the new growth in the spring.

It has large, glossy, green roundish leaves which have up to seven or nine blunt points. The leaves should be sponged occasionally and the plant watered copiously during the summer. It also benefits from standing outside in summer rain from time to time.

Fatshedera lizei is a cross between a fatsia and hedera (ivy) and inherits characteristics from both. Its leaves have the texture and colour of the fatsia but are 'ivy-shaped'.

It grows easily in cold or average rooms, and needs no additional heat in the winter. Keep it out of direct sunlight as this tends to make the leaves wilt. Water it well in the summer, but be careful not to over-water it, which makes the edges of the leaves turn brown. Keep it fairly dry in the winter.

Popular names for *Fatshedera lizei* are the Fat-headed Lizzie or the Ivy Tree. It can grow to a height of eight feet or more, so keep it bushy by pinching out the leader in the spring.

Maranta. Plants in this group are not very easy to grow as they need warmth, shade, root moisture and humidity. These factors, however, make them particularly suitable for bottle gardens and their attractive foliage also gives excitement to the simplest dish garden.

Maranta leuconeura 'Erythrophylla', pictured on page 29 has beautiful leaves with well defined reddish veins and greeny-brown markings. If you attempt to grow it outside a bottle garden, keep it out of draughts in a minimum temperature of 55°F (13°C) and in a shady position with its pot surrounded by damp peat.

Maranta leuconeura 'Kerchoveana' is a particularly unusual plant in that its leaves lift upwards and clasp together at sunset. Because of this it is popularly known as the Prayer Plant. It is very bushy and has prominent brownish black markings on either side of its centre veins. Its growing requirements are the same as the *Maranta leuconeura* 'Erythrophylla'.

Calathea makoyana. The striking markings on the foliage of this plant have earned it its common name of the Peacock Plant. It is best known of the calatheas, all of which have markings rather similar to the Marantas and are sometimes sold by florists as Marantas. *Calathea makoyana* has very lovely silvery-green leaves with veins of dark green and edges of medium green. It is not easy to grow indoors and for this reason is often regarded as an expendable plant which should be replaced every year or so. To flourish it needs humidity and warmth, so again, it does well in a bottle garden.

Slightly easier to grow perhaps, but less colourful is the *Calathea insignis*.

If you want to grow calatheas outside of a bottle garden, plant them in rich open soil – half peat or leaf-mould and half light loam. Keep in a shady place, out of draughts, at a temperature of not less than 60°F (15·5°C). Give them lots of water during the summer and considerably less in the winter. The leaves benefit from being sprayed, and the plant will flourish best if kept in an outer container full of moist peat.

Codiaeum variegatum Pictum is often known as the South Sea Laurel, although the most common name for this plant, and its numerous lovely varieties, is Croton. They are in fact, usually sold under this name. They are gaudy, tropical shrubs with tough evergreen leaves which are deeply veined and vary considerably in shape. Sometimes they are straight, sometimes twisted, and they are patterned with orange, yellow, red, green and black.

Crotons are difficult plants to grow. They require a constant temperature that never falls below 55°F (13°C) and they must be kept out of draughts and bright sunlight. Their need for humidity can be dealt with as previously described. The leaves need frequent syringing and it is advisable to use tepid water when watering.

Other varieties are the *Codiaeum* 'Madame Mayne' which has a predominance of yellow in its leaves, the *Codiaeum* 'Emperor Alexander II', the young leaves of which are yellowy in colour and turn to deep red as they get older, and the *Codiaeum* 'Van Ostense' which is slow-growing but has particularly beautiful dainty narrow, variegated yellow and green leaves.

As Crotons grow old, in common with Cordyline and Ficus, they tend to lose their lower leaves. To avoid having increasingly 'leggy' plants you should 'air-layer' them, as described on page 16.

Dieffenbachia. Plants in this group also tend to shed their lower leaves, and likewise, will benefit from air-layering. Known as Dumb Cane or Mother-in-Law Plant, most dieffenbachias are tall handsome plants with prominently marked leaves. They need fairly high and constant temperatures with good humidity to flourish and although deep shade reduces their variegation, they do best in a slightly shady position. They appear to be unaffected by gas fumes.

Dieffenbachias like to have their leaves syringed regularly during the summer, at which time, they should be kept well watered. Watering must be considerably reduced in the winter, and at no time should they be over-watered.

An unfortunate characteristic of dieffenbachias is that their sap is poisonous. For this reason they should obviously be kept out of the way of children and pets, and are perhaps more suited to office situations than the home. In any event take care when cutting the cane or removing a leaf to see that the sap does not enter a cut on your hands.

Attractive varieties are *Dieffenbachia amoena* which has immense glossy, green leaves with beautiful white 'feathering' markings, *Dieffenbachia picta*, known for its dark green, pointed oblong leaves that are covered with white and pale green spots, and *Dieffenbachia picta* 'Exotica' which has large irregular markings of creamy white.

Philodendrons. This group probably contain some of the best known foliage house plants and they are both bushy and upright, as well as climbing and trailing, varieties. They are valued for the beautiful leaves, which are varied in shape.

Philodendrons probably grow better in the conditions found in modern homes than any other house plant. They survive happily if they are kept warm – ideally in a temperature of not less than 65°F (18°C) – and moderately moist. Keep them out of direct sunlight, and let them dry out between waterings.

Among the bushy types, *Philodendron bipinnatifidum* is an imposing plant, with leaves that can grow to two and a half feet long and one and a half feet wide. Clearly it needs plenty of room for display, but it is easy to grow. It produces long fleshy roots from its growing point, and these should be trained back into the soil.

Others are *Philodendron* 'Burgundy' which is very tolerant and assumes a rich hue from the reflections of the colour of its deep, wine-red stem in its superb two-foot long leaves; *Philodendron dubium*, which is slow-growing and never gets out of hand; *Philodendron wendlandi*, which is a compact plant with long narrow leaves and is very tolerant of extremes of temperature and humidity, and *Philodendron selloum*, which is striking, sturdy and slow-growing with very large leaves cut into strips half-way to the midrib. As the leaves of the latter fall, they leave white scars on the stem, which add to the plant's attractiveness. It is particularly resistant to cold and will stand freezing temperatures.

Cyperus alternifolius is a semi-aquatic plant that originated in the swamps of Madagascar. It can not be over-watered, to the extent that it likes to stand permanently in a saucer of water. It is hardy, easy to grow and perhaps rather oddly in view of its origin, does not need to be kept in a permanently heated room. It also likes

to be in semi-shade.

Its unusual growth produces rosettes of grass-like leaves at its base, from which emanate flowering stems that are surmounted by crowns on shorter leaves. These are reminiscent of the ribs of an umbrella, which accounts for the plant's common name – the Umbrella Plant.

Schefflera actinophylla provides an example of how confusing it can be to call house plants by their common or popular names. Like *Cyperus alternifolius*, its common name is the Umbrella Tree, but the two plants could not be more different from each other. *Schefflera actinophylla* has long, glossy-green, pointed leaves which grow in groups of three or five at the top of individual leaf stems, again like the ribs of an umbrella. It flourishes in almost any conditions, grows quickly and will eventually become very large.

This sort of confusion goes to show that it is better to learn and use the botanical names of plants, long and frightening though some of them may seem. Good florists will use the botanical names.

Peperomias. These moderate to small plants have very lovely leaves. In spite of the fact that they are classed as foliage house plants, they do produce small flowers, which in some varieties are carried high on colourful stalks.

Best known of the peperomias is *Peperomia caperata* which has dark green, crinkled or corrugated leaves that grow on pink stems. It produces large numbers of curious cream-coloured flowers on light brown stalks which curve over at the top and look like miniature shepherd's crooks.

Another variety is *Peperomia magnoliifolia* or *Peperomia obtusifolia* 'Variegata'. It is a tough, slow-growing shrubby plant with brilliant cream and green leaves borne on short, branching, reddish stems.

Perhaps the most beautiful of all is the *Peperomia sandersii*, known as the Watermelon Peperomia, because of the shape of its leaves. These are dark green patterned with crescents of silver.

Peperomia hederifolia is similar to *Peperomia caperata*, but rather larger. Its leaves are less corrugated and a metallic, grey-green colour. It has white or yellowish flowers borne on narrow spikes, and while they are not beautiful, they contrast pleasingly with the plant's massed foliage.

All peperomias require warmth, humidity, some shade and, as they have small roots, they like to be grown in small well-drained pots. Water them frequently in the summer, although be careful not to be too excessive, and keep them rather drier in the winter. Take care not to splash the leaves and crowns when watering as these have a tendency to rot. Peperomias are generally considered suitable components for bottle gardens, and *Peperomia magnoliifolia* is particularly recommended.

Climbing and Trailing Foliage Plants

Before discussing climbing and trailing plants individually, a word should be said about supporting climbers. Those that do not produce aerial roots, such as ivy, can be supported by canes. Push three canes into the soil, close to the edge of the pot. You can then train the stems of the plant to grow round these. If the plants are not self-clinging, tie them to the canes, using the plastic or paper covered wires available on the market. If these are unobtainable, use string, but don't tie it too tightly, or you will restrict the plant's growth.

Plants which do produce aerial roots, that is roots that grow out of the stems above ground level, such as some Philo-dendrons, should be supported by a moss stick, from which these roots can draw supplies of water. To make a moss stick, cut a strip of $\frac{1}{4}$-inch, thirty or thirty-six inch wide plastic mesh, and roll it into a cylinder three inches in diameter. Overlap the edges by about $\frac{3}{4}$-inch. Fasten along the edges at six-inch intervals with wire. Insert two small sticks at right angles to each other through the mesh near the bottom of the cylinder and stand it in the pot on top of a layer of crocks. Soak some shredded moss for about twenty-four hours so it is well moistened and then mix it with an equal amount of vermiculite or similar material. Pack this into the cylinder, pushing it down firmly and stopping about four inches from the top. Put a layer of soil on the crocks, plant the climber and top up the pot with soil.

As the climber grows, train it up the cylinder, holding it in position with U-shaped pieces of wire, inserted on the slant into the moss. Keep the moss moist by inserting a small flowerpot in the top end of the cylinder and topping this up with water daily.

Chlorophytum comosum 'Variegatum' is often regarded as the easiest of foliage house plants to grow indoors and to propa-gate. It grows a dense tuft of arching leaves, rather like grass, that are edged bright green and have a stripe of cream running along the centre. Its insignificant white flowers are produced on long corn-coloured stalks, which stand well above the plant. After flowering, small plantlets develop on the stalks, weighing them down. The resulting pendulous or trailing effect makes it an effective plant to grow in a hanging basket.

The common name for this plant is Spider Plant, and it flourishes best in a bright place, out of direct sunlight and appreciates medium humidity. Keep it reasonably moist, and never allow it to dry out. It is advisable to re-pot it annually, in a slightly larger container each time.

Chlorophytum comosum is propagated by 'layering' – see page 16.

Tradescantias are an easy-to-grow, popular group of trailing plants, of which the *Tradescantia fluminensis* is probably the best known. Commonly called the Wander-ing Jew, Travelling Sailor or Wandering Plant, it has small pointed, striped leaves, which in bright light (although not direct sunlight), may have some pinkish tints.

Attractive varieties of *Tradescantia flu-minensis* are, 'Variegata' which has white stripes on green leaves and 'Aurea' which has yellow striped leaves. The leaves of the

'Aurea' do at times revert to green, in which case the shoots should be cut off as they appear.

Tradescantias flourish in average and warm rooms if given plenty of water in the summer and considerably less in the winter. They like good light, although they will grow in shade. In shady conditions, however, they tend to lose much of their beautiful colour. Most tradescantias become straggly and defoliated with age, particularly if kept in a dry atmosphere. However, they are so easily propagated (see page 18), that this can be easily overcome by replacing them from time to time. They are useful for wall bracket displays, and hanging baskets.

Zebrina pendula is closely related to the tradescantias and was, in fact, formerly known as the *Tradescantia zebrina*. It is a very beautiful, easy-to-grow plant which can be grown in similar conditions, and used in much the same situations, as tradescantias.

The upper surfaces of the leaves of *Zebrina pendula* are silvery, edged green with a purple stripe, while the undersides are bright purple. These colours are greatly accentuated if the plant is kept a little on the dry side.

Zebrina purpusii, formerly known as *Tradescantia purpurea*, is, also very similar, but has dark mauve leaves that are rather larger than most tradescantias. *Cissus antarctica*, or the Kangaroo Vine, is very easy to grow. It is a tough, fast-growing, self-clinging climber, that will,

if permitted, grow to a height of eight feet. It makes an effective plant for forming a light screen or room divider.

The leaves of *Cissus antarctica* are a lovely fresh green colour, oval in shape and well veined. Although it grows best indoors when kept in a good light, out of strong sunlight, it will grow in somewhat sunless, more shady rooms. It is quite tolerant of lower temperatures and thrives at a level of 50°F (10°C), although it likes some humidity. Water it well during the summer, but let it dry out almost completely between waterings. It needs very little water during the winter.

Cissus discolor is an attractive variety of the same genus, but it is rather harder to grow. It has beautiful green, reddish-purple, mottled-white leaves.

Hederas or True Ivies are perhaps the most useful of all climbing and trailing house plants and can be most effectively used for all functions of this type of plant. They can be planted in baskets, grown over the edge of bowls, climb supports of bamboo canes or they can be grown to be used as room dividers.

There are many varieties, of which *Hedera helix* is the most common. It has deep green, shiny leaves and will grow in a moderately dark, shady and cool situation. Other varieties are:

Hedera helix 'Glacier' which has small silvery grey leaves with thin white margins. It is an excellent trailer.

Hedera helix 'Christata' which has pale green leaves that are unusual in the way

they are twisted and crinkled at the edges. It has been likened to parsley, and is also called 'Holly Ivy'. It likes to be kept drier than other varieties.

Hedera helix 'Sagittifolia' whose small dark-green leaves are also unusual. They are comprised of five lobes, the central one of which is sharply pointed and much longer than the others.

There is little difficulty involved in the cultivation of ivies. They like to be grown in small pots, in good moisture retaining soil, which contains some rotted compost or peat. Keep them moist during the summer, never letting them dry out. Keep them out of bright light, away from warm conditions or constantly dry air, and spray their leaves regularly.

Hedera canariensis 'Variegata', or the Canary Island Ivy is another species of *Hedera* that is popular as a house plant. It has large leaves, deep green in the middle and fading to silvery grey with a white margin. It is slower growing and less hardy than *helix* ivies and will certainly die if it is exposed to frost.

A keen indoor gardener with time to spare can create an extremely decorative ivy standard. To do so, cut away all the shoots from a fatshedera, except one which is growing more or less vertically. Stake it and leave it to grow to a height of three to four feet, continuously removing all but the top growth as it grows. Cut off the top of the plant and make a horizontal cut, half an inch deep, across the cross section of the stem. Insert four cuttings of ivy, each four inches long, into this and bind them in with raffia or plastic tape. Tie polythene bags over the top of them and leave until the cuttings have taken, which is usually within eight to ten weeks.

Philodendrons. Plants belonging to this group have already been mentioned in the Bushy and Upright Section; together with the growing conditions most Philodendrons like.

The most popular of the climbing philodendrons is the *Philodendron scandens*, the lovely heart-shaped leaves of which have given it the popular name – 'Sweetheart Vine'. It is considered to be one of the easiest of all house plants to grow and is an excellent plant for a dark room. Although it ideally likes warmth, it will grow reasonably in a cool room and is unaffected by gas and other fumes. It is primarily a climbing plant and throws out many aerial roots. It is therefore ideal for climbing a moss stick (see page 31), but it can be grown as a bushy plant if the leader is regularly pinched out.

A similar, but larger version, *Philodendron cordatum*, or 'Totem Pole Philodendron' is popular in the United States.

Another climbing philodendron is *Philodendron melanochryson*, or *andreanum* as it is known when it becomes adult. It is difficult to grow, but its great beauty issues a tremendous challenge to the ambitious house plant enthusiast. It is a slender climber which produces aerial roots and has spectacular foliage composed of five to six inch long, elongated, heart-shaped leaves. They are dark green with a velvet texture, but their purplish pink undersides make them appear greenish purple.

To flourish, *Philodendron melanochryson* needs a warm humid atmosphere at a temperature of 65°F (18°C). Water sufficiently to keep the soil moist in summer and fairly dry in winter.

Other interesting philodendrons are *Philodendron erubescens* and *Philodendron leichtlinii*. The former has arrow shaped leaves, which in a young plant have a rosy tinge, but in an older plant become dark green with a purplish tinge. It has aerial roots and is fairly easy to grow in average or warm conditions, but it should be remembered that it is a large plant.

Philodendron leichtlinii is a slender climber with fantastic, evenly slashed, oval leaves. It is difficult to grow and needs more heat and humidity than can be comfortably supplied in most living rooms.

Rhoicissus rhomboidea is a climber and/or trailer which has much the same glossy, green veined foliage as *Cissus antarctica*. It is distinguishable by its leaflets, which emerge from the stem in groups of three at one point, and not singly at intervals along the stalk as in the *Cissus antarctica*. It also has very attractive silvery buds and tendrils and is effective as a screen or room divider.

It is an easy-to-grow plant, liking good light, but not direct sunlight. It is happiest in a centrally-heated room, but is tolerant of averagely warm temperatures. Water it freely in the summer, and more moderately in the winter. It grows quickly, so keep it under control by pinching out the growing tips of its tallest stems.

Ficus pumila is an attractive small hardy climbing or trailing plant which has small bright green leaves with darker coloured veins. It is a 'beginner's' plant as it is so easy to grow. It prefers cool or average rooms and a shady position. It likes moist air, however, and needs to be kept well-watered even in the winter. In fact the soil must never be allowed to dry out. It appears to be unaffected by gas and other fumes.

Ficus pumila produces aerial roots which will cling to a moss stick or even just to a rough surface such as a piece of bark or the outside walls of a container. It is just as effective grown as a trailer and is ideal for hanging baskets or for growing over the edge of a dish.

Another of the Ficus genus, *Ficus radicans* 'Variegata' is a beautiful plant with small slender-pointed leaves marked with cream. It is difficult to grow, needing a constant temperature that never falls below 50°F (10°C) and a very moist atmosphere. A lovely plant for a hanging basket, it can also be grown as a bushy plant by pinching out the shoot tips as they appear.

Syngonium podophyllum. This is a very attractive plant, with three-pronged arrowhead-like, cream-tinted leaves. It throws out aerial roots and is happiest when climbing a moss stick. It makes an ideal centre piece in a dish garden.

It grows pretty well in warm or average rooms, under normal household conditions.

Let the soil dry out between waterings.

Scindapsus aureus or Devil's Ivy can quite excusably be mistaken for a variegated philodendron. Its variegated green and yellow leaves are heart-shaped, but its foliage tends to be a little larger and more lush than most philodendrons, particularly if its many aerial roots are trained on a moss stick. It is also a lovely plant to trail over the edge of a dish garden, although it is undoubtedly happier when grown on its own.

It is not an easy plant to keep and grows best in slight shade in the summer with stronger light in the winter. It likes a warm, draught-free position and a moist atmosphere. If the leaves of a young plant turn brown at the edges, do not be too worried. If well cared for, this is overcome as the plant becomes established.

A particularly beautiful variety is the 'Marble Queen', which has cream leaves flecked with green. It is a slow grower and although it likes full light, it must be kept away from direct sunlight or its leaves will turn green all over.

Ferns and Palms

There are several thousand species of fern, but only a very small proportion can be persuaded to grow indoors. A number of these, however, grow easily and are effective in a room as single specimens or as members of a group display. They seem to be happiest when grown only with other ferns.

Ferns need good light, but mostly abhor bright sunlight and usually like to be kept in a warm place in temperatures which do not fall below 50°F (10°C). They require a moist atmosphere and like to grow with their pots contained in moist peat. For this reason, some of the smaller ferns are excellent for bottle gardens. They like a rich loam, which contains at least fifty per cent peat. This should be kept well watered during the growing period and much drier when the plant is resting. Ferns should never be subjected to a hot, dry atmosphere, particularly if gas fumes are present. Such conditions will turn the tips of the fronds brown.

Asparagus Fern, (*Asparagus plumosus* and *Asparagus sprengeri*) are not in fact true ferns but are regarded as such by most people. They have feathery foliage and are climbing plants, but can be kept reasonably low by pinching out new growth. Asparagus fern is treasured by flower arrangers because it makes such attractive accompanying foliage.

Asplenium nidus avis, known as Bird's Nest Fern, is one of the most striking of all indoor ferns. It is characterized by its glossy, bright-green, fronds with slightly undulated margins, set in a way that has been likened to a shuttlecock. Its leaves grow eventually to about twenty-four inches long and three to eight inches wide. In common with other ferns, it does not like bright sun, but it does need more light and warmth than most.

Nephrolepsis exalta is one of the most beautiful ferns. It has cascading fronds

that can grow as long as three feet, and have three inch long leaflets all along them. It likes a good deal of water through the year and repays attention with a permanent fountain of rich green foliage. It has a multiplicity of popular names, among them the Boston Fern, Curly Fern, Crested Ladder Fern and Whitsun Fern.

Cyrtomium falcatum is valuable because it grows well in an ordinary living room, providing it does not cool to too great an extent at night. It has shiny, dark green, toothed leaves that contrast well with more delicate-looking ferns.

Palms, particularly when young, make good house plants, with their plumes of beautiful green leaves. Most of them must be sited in a place with plenty of light, but they can manage without sunlight. They grow best if kept slightly pot bound, but should be 'top-dressed' each spring (see page 14). They need good drainage, generous watering in the summer and must be kept out of draughts. Watering should be considerably reduced in the winter during which time the temperature should not fall below 50°F (10°C).

Neanthe bella is one of the best palms for growing indoors. It is relatively small, reaching an ultimate height of 4 feet and it is easy to grow. It has long pinnate leaves which are bright green and hang gracefully. It grows in the conditions already outlined, and in addition appreciates having its leaves sprayed occasionally.

Howea forsteriana, or Kentia, Flat or Thatch Leaf Palm is also a good palm for house cultivation. It will, however, ultimately grow to a height of six feet. Another of the same species, the *Howea belmoreana* or Curly Palm is a rather slower grower and also more elegant. Both have graceful pendulous, feathery leaves. They need a winter temperature of not less than 45°F (7°C).

Chamaerops humilis or Fan Palm is hardy and easy to grow. It is happiest in cool or only moderately warm rooms. It is an evergreen shrub growing up to eight feet tall and produces a clump of stiff, fan-shaped leaves on long stems.

Phoenix roebelinii is a species of palm often seen in florists. It is very elegant and a striking house plant, with feathery dark green leaves that have leaflets, which are sometimes sickle-shaped. The richness of its colour can be retained by putting a lump of sulphate of iron on the surface of the soil and allowing it to dissolve during the course of watering. *Phoenix roebelinii* needs to be kept warm and in a temperature that does not fall below 60°F (15°C).

Plants for Flowers

Flowering plants grown for indoor use are usually divided into two categories – flowering house plants and flowering pot plants. The essential difference between them is that the foliage of flowering house plants remains alive and attractive throughout the year, even when they are not in flower, whereas the leaves of pot plants usually fall after the flowers fade. It is only when pot plants are in flower, therefore, that they have any decorative value. Most pot plants are discarded when they have finished flowering, but with care and attention, some can be preserved to flower again the following year.

In spite of the relatively short life of flowering pot plants, they are a very worthwhile addition to the home. They flower for quite a long time, often in otherwise rather dreary winter months, and the beauty of their flowers often outshines those of flowering house plants.

Like foliage house plants, some types of flowering house plants are bushy, while others are trailers or climbers, and they thrive in a variety of conditions, which will again be discussed individually in this chapter. One rule that may be applied generally, to flowering house plants, however, is that most of them bloom better when the size of their pot is restricted.

Begonias. There are many types of begonia that make popular, easy-to-grow flowering pot plants. Generally, they like a well-lit place, that has a moist atmosphere and is well away from gas fumes. Water them well during their growing season, and keep them

Preceding pages
(left) Euphorbia pulcherrima
(right) Stephanotis floribunda

fairly dry when they are resting. In winter they like a constant temperature of about 50°–55°F (10°–13°C).

An attractive climbing begonia is the *Begonia scandens* 'Glaucophylla'. It has shiny, pointed, greyish-green leaves that make a lovely foil for its brick-red pendulous flower clusters. It makes a superb room divider if allowed to clamber up some trellis structure. It flowers in the winter, dislikes hot rooms, but appreciates a moist atmosphere.

Begonia maculata is a bushy plant with decorative, large leaves that are brightly spotted with silver. It produces pendulous bunches of bright-pink flowers for long periods at almost any time of year.

Begonia manicata is a winter-blooming begonia with erect stems that bear small rose-pink flowers.

Begonia semperflorens is probably the most widely grown indoor begonia. It can flower the whole year round, and is a sun-lover and fume-hater! Water it freely throughout the summer, without wetting its leaves and reduce watering considerably in the winter, when the temperature should be constant at about 50°–55°F (10°–13°C).

Flower colours range from white and pink, to red and crimson and the leaves can be green or reddy brown. Interesting cultivars are 'Aloha' which has salmon-orange flowers and 'Curly Locks' which has dark copper leaves and pink blooms, crested with yellow.

Hoya carnosa is a lovely climbing plant with glossy oval, slender-pointed fleshy leaves and clusters of waxen, star-shaped pinkish-white, sweetly scented flowers. Picturesquely, drops of nectar are often to be found hanging from their reddish pink centres. The plant blooms in the summer, at which time it likes warmth and plenty of water. It also appreciates an occasional feed of liquid manure when it is growing. As soon as the buds appear however, feeding should be stopped and watering considerably reduced.

A beautiful variegated variety is the *Hoya carnosa*, 'Variegata', which is a rather slower grower, but has lovely cream and green leaves. Another attractive species is *Hoya australis* which has white flowers tinged with pink. It has a fragrance resembling that of honeysuckle.

Jasmine. There are two equally lovely jasmines – *Jasminum polyanthum* and *Jasminum primulinum* – that will flower in the house, particularly if they are kept in an atmosphere that is warm and fairly moist. Both like to be kept in a sunny place and in a winter temperature that does not fall below 45°F (7°C). Under these conditions, they are both evergreen and, as climbers, can be kept under control by stopping the new shoots during the growing season.

Jasminum polyanthum resembles the white garden jasmine and has white, highly perfumed spring flowers, that are tinged pink on the outside.

Jasminum primulinum also blooms in spring, or even earlier and has bright yellow, semi-double flowers. These show up magnificently against the plant's dark green, trifoliate leaves. Supported on a framework, *Jasminum primulinum* makes a good room divider.

Passiflora caerulea is a quick growing, hardy climber, popularly known as Passion Flower. The flower filaments, that bloom in the summer, are violet-blue with whitish sepals. There is also a pure white variety – 'Constance Elliott', and other species which have red-pink and purplish flowers.

Passiflora caerulea likes a sunny position, and plenty of water, with an occasional feed, during the summer. In winter the temperature should not fall below 50°F (10°C), and it dislikes coal and gas fires. Keep it under control by pruning it hard in the early spring, but it looks particularly attractive trained up two canes set at an angle, so that its stems make a bridge across the top.

Columnea banksii. This is harder to grow, but a very attractive flowering house plant. Keep it in a warm room, where the winter temperature does not fall below 55°F (13°C). Water it well during its growing period, but not so the soil is continuously saturated. Provide the humidity it likes by surrounding its pot with moist peat, and keep it in a well lit place, out of direct sunlight.

Although it is possible to tie some species of Columnea to supports and train them as climbers, they are really happier as trailers. Its flowers are reddish-orange and tubular shaped. They are about three inches long and grow either side of pendulous stems.

Stephanotis floribunda is an extremely beautiful, highly perfumed vigorous climber. Its white waxy flowers are similar to those of *Jasminum polyanthum* which, together with the fact that it is a native of Madagascar, have earned it its common name – Madagascar Jasmine. The flowers grow in clusters along the length of its stems, which need supporting, and the evergreen leaves make an attractive foil for the fresh blooms.

It is not an easy plant to grow. Keep it in a place that gives it good light and warmth, and make sure the winter temperature does not fall below 55°F (13°C). Grow it in a pot with good drainage, and surrounded by damp peat to provide a moist atmosphere. Spraying it occasionally is also beneficial.

Aeschyanthus speciosus can either be grown as a climber, by supporting it with short pea sticks or bamboo canes, or as a trailer in a pot or hanging basket. It is a beautiful plant for indoor decoration, its long stems bearing lovely, fleshy, deep-green, narrow leaves and clusters of orange, tubular, fragrant flowers. These appear in the summer, but the plant should not be allowed to flower during its first season.

Plant it in a rich mixture of silted leafmould, and a little sphagnum moss. Keep it well watered in the summer and reasonably dry during the winter, when the temperature should be about 50°F (10°C). It likes good drainage, and should be re-potted annually.

Impatiens petersiana. Commonly known as Busy Lizzie, this is a plant that flowers nearly the whole year round, and is renownedly easy and quick to grow. It is

available in dwarf forms, such as 'Baby Grange' and 'Baby Scarlet', and in a number of taller varieties, of which 'Red Herald', with its large scarlet flowers marked with white is particularly attractive. Flower colours among impatiens and its hybrids range from orange, red, pink and white to carmine and violet.

Keep it in a sunny place while it is flowering, and in a well-lit place, but out of the sun at other times. It likes warmth in the winter, with just enough water to prevent the leaves wilting. In summer it likes lots of water and feeding, and also overhead spraying. Don't do this in the winter, however, when it is subject to attacks of mildew. Keep plants bushy, by periodically pinching out new growth.

Anthurium scherzerianum is a rather difficult to grow, but impressive, houseplant. It needs to be kept in a centrally-heated room at a constant temperature of 60°F (15°C), in a well-drained pot, surrounded by damp peat to keep the atmosphere moist. Water it well in the summer and spray it frequently with tepid water. In the winter, reduce the amount of surrounding peat, but make sure the soil never dries out.

Anthurium scherzerianum repays care and attention with its wonderful, wax-like, flamboyant, scarlet flowers. They grow on tall red stems and are composed of a spathe about three inches long, and a spirally-twisted orange-red spadix. The lanceolate leaves are long and slender and shiny.

Beloperone guttata. An easy-to-grow flowering house plant, commonly known as the Shrimp Plant. This is doubtless because of its rather unusual pink flowers and bracts, which are reminiscent of shrimps in shape and colour. They grow at the end of arching stems, laden with medium-green coloured leaves.

This plant flourishes in a sunny position with plenty of watering and regular feeding in spring and summer. When the weather is hot, spray it occasionally. Keep it dry and cool in the winter. Spring pruning will encourage new growth, and pinching out the tops keeps plants bushy. It has become an extremely popular house plant, probably because it is attractive and unusual, and yet, easy to grow.

Clivia miniata is another easy-to-grow flowering house plant, which is claimed to be as tough and long lasting as the Aspidistra. Popularly known as the Kaffir Lily, it has orange or red funnel-shaped flowers that appear in the spring among its fleshy, strap-like green leaves.

It likes lots of light, but not direct sunlight, plenty of water and feeding in the summer and its leaves washed and syringed during warm weather. Winter temperatures should not be below 45°–50°F (7°–10°C), and it should be kept fairly dry. It dislikes having its roots disturbed, and blooms best when pot-bound, so re-pot it only when it is absolutely necessary.

Saintpaulia ionantha, or African Violet, is a favourite among house plants. It is a dainty, low-growing plant, that forms clumps of velvety, rounded hair-covered, distinctly veined leaves, that are dark green, and sometimes purple on their undersides. The flowers resemble violets and have a brilliant mass of yellow stamens. According to the plant variety, the colour of the flowers may be pure white, all shades of pink and mauve or the deepest purple and violet. They stay on the plant for many months.

In spite of its popularity, the African Violet is not an easy plant to grow and its demands are extremely exacting. Its first requirement, is a temperature that never falls below 60°F (15°C) and is not subject to fluctuations. It needs a moist atmosphere, which may be provided as previously described and it needs plenty of water, seemingly all the time as it does not appear to have a resting period. Water it from below, or with a very narrow-spouted watering can, because its foliage, stalks and crowns will rot if they get wet. Give it regular doses of liquid feed, and make sure it is not exposed to draughts or gas fumes.

Even its light requirements are exacting – keep it in good light, but not direct sunlight. It has, in fact, been established that saintpaulias need fourteen hours of light during each twenty-four hours. In winter, anyway, this must be partly natural and partly artificial.

Aphelandra squarrosa 'Louisae' is another rather difficult to grow, but very showy, plant, which is well worth some perseverance on the part of the indoor gardener. It is a beautiful plant, with ten-inch long, pointed, very dark-green leaves, the veins of which are boldly delineated in pale cream. These have doubtless given it its popular name of Zebra Plant. In addition it has spectacular yellow flower bracts, each segment of which produces an ivory, tubular-shaped flower.

It has been found that younger plants are more adaptable to house conditions than older ones. In either event, it needs to be in a well-lit, but not sun-lit, spot in which there is always moist and warm air. Its soil should be kept constantly moist in the summer, but not soggy, and on the dry side in the winter. Spray the foliage from time to time, and remove the flowers when they have faded.

Billbergia are bromeliads, (a large family of herbaceous plants, originating mostly from the tropical parts of America), that are popular and easy-to-grow. They have narrow, twelve-inch long, evergreen leaves, at the base of which rosettes form. Long stalks carrying colourful exotic-looking blooms at their ends, grow from the rosettes. The flowers are composed of large conspicuous rosy bracts and small, yellowish green flowers.

Billbergias tolerate cool winter conditions, dry air, and to a certain extent, gas fumes. They should be kept in a place with good light, and some warmth will encourage them to flower. Do not over-water, and give them liquid feed while they are growing.

Aechmeas are also bromeliads and are frequently cultivated as houseplants. They are characterized by the large strap-like leaves that form a vase-like rosette at their base.

They are adaptable to cool and warm conditions, and do well in most rooms, provided they are kept in comparatively small pots and are given good light. Keep them relatively dry in the winter, and don't water them too heavily in summer. You should keep their central 'vase-like' cavity topped up with water, however, and if possible this should be rain water.

The varieties most frequently seen growing indoors are:

Aechmea fulgens, which has olive-green leaves, with a base of reddish-purple, and produces small blue-petalled flowers that grow from a red calyx; and *Aechmea fasciata*, which has a rosette of leaves, striped in bands of grey and green, with small pink flowers growing from pink bracts. In both cases the flowers do not last very long, but the calyxes and bracts remain colourful for a long time. Neither plant is tall, but can grow up to two feet across.

Vriesia splendens is another bromeliad and is very hardy. It has twelve- to sixteen-inch long, upright green leaves, slightly curved back at the tip, with blackish cross-bands on either side. These form a funnel-shaped rosette with a central vase, that like the *Aechmeas*, should be kept constantly filled with water. From this, there emerges a flower spike, which bears at its top, a bright scarlet, spear-shaped bract, often at least two feet long. Tubular flowers grow at the base of the bracts and although they do not last for long, the bracts keep their brilliance for some time.

Vriesia splendens likes the same conditions and treatment as an Aechmea. It will tolerate a dark corner, but prefers to stand in good light and likes a winter temperature of not less then 55°F (13°C).

Citrus mitis, known also as the Calamondin Orange Tree, is an unusual house plant, in that it often bears flowers and fruit simultaneously. It has dainty, white, frarant flowers, and small, colourful oranges. These are edible, but rather sour.

Citrus mitis, together with other orange species is not difficult to grow. Most of all it needs plenty of sunshine, and it likes ample watering and regular feeding during the summer. Syringe its leaves during hot summer weather, and if you like you can stand it outside from June until the weather turns cold. Keep it fairly dry in the winter, and in a temperature of not less than 50°F (10°C).

Hibiscus rosa-sinensis. This is a bushy plant with dark-green, glossy leaves and large, trumpet-shaped flowers that measure up to five inches across. The flowers can be white, varying shades of pink, red, orange and yellow, and may be single or double blooms.

A very pretty cultivar is *Hibiscus rosa-sinensis* 'Cooperi', which has variegated leaves of deep green and light yellow, tinged reddish-pink. Its flowers, which tend to be less numerous than some other varieties, are red.

Hibiscus thrive in well-lit rooms and when they are in flower, they like to be in full sun. Keep them well watered in the summer and give them occasional feeds of liquid manure. They like to be kept drier in the winter and in a temperature that does not fall below 50°F (10°C). Prune them in early spring as this stimulates bud production. Once the buds form, do not move the plant.

Spathiphyllum wallisii is an elegant flowering house plant, somewhat similar to the Arum Lily. It is an evergreen, with attractive, bright, shiny-green, lance-shaped leaves that grow six to ten inches long. The delicate white flower is carried on a thin stalk rising up through the leaves and surrounded by a white or green spathe. Lasting about a month, the flowers are light green to begin with, then they turn to white and finally revert to green again.

Spathiphyllum wallisii is fairly easy to grow in a warm, shady position with good humidity. It delights in central heating and does not object to deep shade. However, it doesn't like sunlight which turns its foliage yellow.

A larger but otherwise similar variety is *Spathiphyllum wallisii* 'Mauna Loa'.

Callistemon citrinus is a beautiful evergreen shrub, originating from Australia. The variety 'Splendens' has brilliant scarlet flowers, with very colourful long stamens and it blooms over a long period of time. It flourishes in cool conditions and should be top-dressed only, as it grows best when somewhat pot bound. It is commonly known as the Bottle Brush Plant.

Nerium oleander is a shrub requiring plenty of space. It is a beautiful, willow-leaved plant, with clusters of fragrant tubular flowers, measuring at least three inches across. However, every part of it is poisonous – positively deadly if eaten! The most usual colour of the flowers is pink, but there are white, yellow and red varieties, and one species has variegated leaves.

Nerium oleander likes a sunny position with generous watering using tepid water, spraying, and occasional feeding during the summer. Stand it outside as often as possible in the summer, too, as this ripens its wood. In the winter it likes to be in temperatures of no less than 50°F (10°C).

Campanula isophylla is a charming plant, sometimes classed as a trailer, because of its prostrate habit, and it does look particularly lovely if allowed to hang over the edge of a pot. It has delicate flowers that may be white or lilac-blue.

Campanula isophylla 'Mayi' is a beautiful variety, with variegated foliage and delightful china-blue flowers.

Unlike the majority of the members of its large family, *Campanula isophylla*, is not hardy, and should be kept in a place that is cool, well-lit and airy, but free from draughts. Give it plenty of water during the summer, while it is growing, and keep it rather dry in the winter. Winter temperatures should be kept fairly constant at 45°– 50°F (7°–10°C). If you 'dead-head' *Campanula isophylla* regularly, it will remain in flower for a long time.

Flowering Pot Plants

The most crucial period in the life of a flowering pot plant is during the first few days after it has been bought. Usually the supplier has not kept it under normal house conditions, in which case it would be a mistake to install it immediately in a warm room. Instead put it in a cool, light place where the temperature is about 50°F (10°C) for a week or so. Give it very little water during this time, although it will benefit from spraying with tepid water. You can then move it to a warmer room, but if it begins to wilt, give it a few more days in the cool place.

Azalea indica. The many varieties of Indian azalea are often described as the most 'valuable' of flowering pot plants, because they are laden with red, pink or white blooms during the cheerless winter months. As a section of the rhododendron family, the azalea is a shrub with small evergreen leaves and the varieties and hybrids of *Rhododendron indicum* and *Rhododendron simsii* form the bulk of those grown as house plants.

Azalea indica is not always found to be easy to grow, because it must have moist air, no draughts and a fairly warm and steady temperature. It is most likely to flourish if kept in a well-lit airy spot, away from direct sunlight. Water it by standing the pot up to its rim in water for a period of time, and feed it regularly during its blooming season. If you remove the flower heads as soon as they die, the flowering season will be lengthened.

Azalea indica can be preserved through the summer by 'planting' the pot in the ground out of doors in May, after the danger of frost has passed. It can remain out of doors until the autumn, when you should re-pot it and bring it back indoors. A good potting medium is lime-free sterilized soil containing a proportion of pine-needle peat. *Pelargoniums* are a great favourite among flowering pot plants, the easiest to grow of which is the *Pelargonium zonale* or Geranium. There are, however, many varieties with a wide range of flower colours and leaf patterns, including some miniatures which do not exceed three inches in height. The more vigorous cultivars can be trained on trellis to form colourful room dividers.

The ivy geraniums – *Pelargonium peltatum* – are excellent for hanging baskets, but not as easy to grow as bush plants.

The needs of the *Pelargonium zonale* are pure air and a warm, sunlit, dry, airy position. A window-sill facing south is ideal. Water and feed freely in the summer, and dead head regularly to encourage continual flowering.

The illustration opposite shows a *Pelargonium domesticum*. It is derived from various species, which produce gorgeous close-packed clusters of large beautifully marked flowers in many shades of pink, cerise, red and maroon, varying in intensity to almost black.

Chrysanthemum. Modern lighting makes it possible to have potted chrysanthemums in flower throughout the year. Furthermore, although naturally dwarf plants exist, by using dwarfing compounds, nurserymen can offer pot versions of many of the taller, garden varieties.

Chrysanthemums need to be in cool, well lit, but sunless places where there is a good air circulation. Water them regularly to ensure the soil does not dry out. Once the potted varieties stop flowering, they are usually discarded, but if you plant them in the garden, they will subsequently grow to their normal height.

Begonias. Besides varieties of foliage and flowering house plants already discussed, there are some species of begonia which are classified as flowering pot plants. These include most of the hybrid and tuberous begonias, which provide a superb summer and autumn display, and varieties such as the Christmas Begonia and Gloire de Lorraine, which flower in the winter.

All these begonias are fairly easy to grow and should be kept in a room where the light is good and the temperature is not lower than 55°F (13°C). Water them freely when they are in flower. Tubers of the tuberous begonias can be kept from year to year and replanted at the appropriate time.

Primula. This popular group of flowering pot plants has a number of attractive species, all of which have a lengthy flowering season. There is a range of colours, even among the common ones – *Primula kewensis* has small, scented, deep yellow flowers; those of *Primula malacoides* are small and light purple; *Primula obconica* has large rose, blue, red, white or salmon-pink blooms, and *Primula sinensis* has large flowers that may be pink, lilac or white.

To grow successfully, primulas need a well-lit, draught free spot, away from heat and direct sunlight. Give them plenty of water during flowering and dead-head them regularly to ensure a long succession of blooms. They also like regular feeding. Normally primulas are discarded after flowering, but *Primula obconica* and *Primula sinensis* can be kept from one season to another by allowing them to remain perpetually in a cool, bright room. Note that the leaves of *Primula obconica* are known to give a skin rash to some people.

Solanum capsicastrum is a gay, delightful shrub, variously known as the Winter, Jerusalem, or Christmas Cherry. It is most cherished for its charming display of shiny orange or red berries which cheer up any room during the winter. It also has pretty white flowers.

Solanum capsicastrum like a cool, but moist atmosphere, and a light position away from draughts and gas fumes. In these conditions, the berries will remain on the bush for months. Water and spray it regularly, and whilst it is berried, give it feeds of liquid manure. If the soil becomes waterlogged, or dried out, the leaves will fall.

It is usual to buy these shrubs fresh each year, but if you prune them back hard and plant them in the garden during the summer, they will usually survive to the following winter.

Camellia. These evergreen, hardy shrubs with their handsome, glossy, dark-green leaves and beautifully coloured, luxuriant, waxen blooms have all the qualities of flowering house plants, but are more commonly classified as flowering pot plants.

It is a good idea to buy a well-budded plant just after Christmas as it is likely to remain in flower for the next two months or so. After this keep it in a cool place and plant it out when there is no more fear of frost.

Camellias like much the same conditions as Indian azaleas, thriving particularly well on the sill of a north facing window, providing it is not draughty. Keep them perpetually moist, and away from draughts, dryness and cold which will make their buds drop.

Achimenes are very beautiful, tuberous, summer-flowering pot plants that are easy to grow. There are a number of hybrids, which have funnel-shaped flowers that grow from the axils of their leaves and may be white, red or violet in colour.

Achimenes need a warm, well-lit place out of direct sunlight. Water them moderately, taking care not to wet their flowers or foliage. Keep their pots in damp peat to provide the moist atmosphere they like.

Buy small tubers in early spring and plant them half-an-inch deep in potting compost. Keep them in a temperature of 65°F (18°C) to start them into growth, and stake the plants' slender stalks as they grow. Once they have flowered, leave them to dry out, then cut down the stems and remove the tubers for re-potting the following spring. Other names for *Achimenes* are Cupid's Bower and Hot-water Plant.

Poinsettia, (Euphorbia pulcherrima). This is rather difficult to grow, but very beautiful, winter flowering pot plant. It has long been a traditional Christmas plant in the United States, and has now become very popular in Great Britain as well. Its most noteworthy feature it its large star-shaped groups of scarlet bracts, often mistaken for flowers, but which in fact surround the insignificant small yellow flowers. The bracts contrast dramatically with the plant's dark-green pointed leaves.

The old varieties of this plant were usually rather straggly, and had a tendency to leaf fall if the growing conditions were not quite right. These problems have been overcome to some degree, and as a result, modern varieties are generally more compact growing. Poinsettias are at their best if they are kept in a moist, fairly warm place with good light, and free from draughts and gas fumes. Spray the leaves occasionally and water plants carefully, never allowing them to become water-logged.

Cyclamen persicum, known too as the Persian Violet is another winter-flowering pot plant. It has lovely heart-shaped grey, green, silver or mottled leaves and a profusion of white, pink, salmon-pink, crimson or cerise flowers. Ranking with an azalea for beauty, it remains in flower long after the azalea has faded.

Not everybody find cyclamen easy to grow. It likes a dry atmosphere with a temperature that does not rise above 50°F (10°C). It needs to be in good light, away from draughts and should be regularly watered by standing the pot in water up to its brim, so that the crown of the plant is never wetted. Feed it and dead-head it regularly while in flower.

To keep it to the following winter, when it stops flowering, stop feeding it and water it less. Put the pot out in the garden in a shady place in the spring and bring it back into the house in late summer. If it needs re-potting, the corm should stand out slightly above the surface. Use a lime-free compost.

Coleus is usually classified as a flowering pot plant, which is perhaps something of an anomaly as its flowers are rather un-interesting, and should really be picked off to divert the energy into its leaves. A justification for discussing it in the 'flower-ing' section, is that the intensity and varia-tion of its beautiful, multi-coloured leaves rival the beauty of many flowering plants!

Coleus are often considered difficult to grow as they need a well-lit, draught-free position, with a moist atmosphere and a temperature that never falls below 55°F (13°C).

Gloxinia is also rather difficult to grow, but it is so lovely that it is well worth some perseverance. There are many varieties, all of which have brilliantly coloured trumpet-shaped flowers and very beautiful, broad, pointed, downy mid-green leaves. The blooms vary in colour from rich crimson, deep red, white and violet to various com-binations of such colours.

As the Gloxinia is usually a greenhouse plant, when it is grown in the house, it needs a warm spot, out of full sunlight, with a moist atmosphere. Keep the soil perpetu-ally moist, and water it with tepid water from the bottom, as the flowers and foliage will be damaged if they are wetted. You should also feed it regularly during its flowering time.

Cineraria (Senecio cruentus) is a popular shrub that is easy to grow. It has large, pale-green leaves and daisy-like flowers of almost every colour except yellow. These appear in winter and spring and are extremely decorative.

Cineraria thrive in a cool, draught-free position with good light, but not direct sunlight. Water them frequently and feed occasionally while they are in flower. Spraying with water eliminates the green-fly which are attracted to them. *Cineraria* are discarded after flowering.

Hydrangea is a beautiful plant that grows to bush proportions out of doors, but can be successfully grown in a pot indoors during its flowering season. It is very decorative with large dramatic heads of white, pink or blue flowers and pleasing green leaves.

To be at their best, hydrangeas should be kept in a fairly warm, draught-free, well-lit place, out of direct sunlight. Water them generously and feed occasionally while they are flowering. When flowering has finished, hydrangeas can be planted out in the garden, but once out of doors, it is un-likely to bloom for two seasons.

Plants from Bulbs

Growing bulbs in containers indoors is a lovely way of bringing spring into the house while winter lingers on outside. Colourful displays of fresh, bright daffodils and narcissi, stately tulips or enchanting crocuses do much to cheer up a room, and hyacinths, which are available in such a variety of colours, can pervade the whole house with their sweet fragance.

A pleasing aspect of growing bulbs indoors is that, provided you plant them in the specially prepared bulb fibre, no drainage is necessary as it is when growing most house plants. Therefore you can use all sorts of gay and unusual pots and bowls and containers to complement your particular decor.

Some people are eminently successful in growing bulbs, while others have repeatedly unsatisfactory results. There is little magic in successful bulb growing, however, and good results can usually be attained by following a few simple rules carefully.

The kind of bulbs you buy is important, and you should only purchase those of first-class quality. Those that are sold to bloom on Christmas Day have been specially cultivated and stored under controlled conditions of humidity and temperature, which develop the embryo bud in the bulb. These bulbs must be bought and planted four months before Christmas if they are to fulfil their promise.

Although there is some variation in method when planting bulbs in containers, (these will be discussed later under the bulb concerned), it is possible to lay down a fairly standard planting procedure that should be successful for most bulbs. First of all, pour moist – but not soggy – bulb fibre in the container to a height that will support a bulb standing on it at the correct level on completion of planting. This varies slightly with the different species – hyacinths, daffodils and narcissi should have their 'noses' just visible; tulips need to be just covered, and small bulbs, (such as crocus), should have their tips a quarter- to half-an-inch below the surface of the fibre.

Place the bulbs on the fibre, a little way from the edge of the bowl, fairly close together, but not touching one another or the bowl. Pack the spaces between the bulbs and the sides of the bowl with moist fibre, and then finish filling the bowl with fibre to the necessary height (see above). Firm the fibre by gently pressing with your fingers and put the bowl in a cool dark place. Leave it for about eight to ten weeks, or in the case of crocuses and other small bulbs, until the buds just show colour. The 'place' could be a cool, shady spot in the garden, in which case you must cover the bowl with a few inches of moist, but not wet, peat, sand or soil. Alternatively, place the bowl in a wooden box and cover it with sand. In both cases, first put the bowl in a well-perforated plastic bag or wrap it in newspaper to keep the fibre clean.

Those who have little or no garden can equally as well keep the bulbs in a cool, dark cupboard or cellar, (coolness is the important factor), or bury them in a box of moist sand as described previously, and keep this on a balcony or paved area. Failing all else, keep the container in a dark corner covered with an upturned cardboard box or a black, polythene tent.

After spending the appropriate time in the dark, transfer the bulbs, which will have one- to two-inch long, blanched shoots to a cool, shady place indoors. The young growth will green up and a week later, you can move them to their permanent position. This should be a warmer, lighter, draught-free spot, that is not near a fire or radiator.

From then on, and during flowering, water the bulbs freely and turn the bowl regularly so that all parts of the plant get equal light. Quite often you will find it is necessary to stake bulbs, particularly perhaps, tulips and hyacinths whose heavy blooms tend to weigh down their stems.

There are various other methods of indoor bulb cultivation as well. Hyacinths and crocuses for instance, can be grown in the familiar, specially-designed, bulb glasses, which have an annular shelf in the upper portion on which the bulb rests. The lower part is filled with water, containing a few pieces of charcoal, at first to a level that touches the bulb, and the glass is then kept in the dark for about eight weeks, by which time the roots will have formed. From then onwards, the water level is lowered so that there is an air space above it, which prevents the bulb rotting. The glass should be kept in semi-shade for a few days and then moved to a lighter place.

A type of bunch-flowered narcissi can be

grown on pebbles in water. In early autumn put a layer of pebbles in a bowl so that they come two inches below its rim. Put the bulbs on top and wedge more pebbles between them for support, until the container is nearly filled. Pour in water (ideally use rainwater, but in any event it should contain a little charcoal), to a level, just below the bottom of the bulbs. Put the container in a cool place – about 45°F (7°C), (it can be dark or light), for about six months. After this, transfer the container and plants to an airy position on a window-sill where there is a steady temperature of 50°–55°F (10°–13°C), but not near a radiator. By mid-winter, the bulbs should be in full bloom and will continue to flower for some time.

Most commonly grown bulbs are expendable and only serve to give an indoor display once, after which they can be planted in the garden. A few can remain as permanent house plants, and examples of both are discussed below.

Crocuses. The large flowering types are suitable and very attractive for indoor culture. Those that are to flower in the spring, must be planted the previous autumn, and those that are to flower in the autumn, must be planted late the previous spring. Both spring and autumn flowering bulbs flower five months after they were planted. Plant as described on page 60 and keep them in their cool place until the buds just show colour.

Snowdrops can be successfully grown indoors and make a delicate, charming display. Plant them in late summer to flower in mid-winter, as described on page 60.

Hyacinths. If you want these to flower in mid-winter, plant the specially prepared bulbs in summer, and for flowering during early spring, plant the bulbs in autumn. When hyacinth bulbs are first planted, they should be kept covered in a cool place where the temperature does not exceed 45°–50°F (7°–10°C). After about seven weeks, there will be sufficient growth to allow you to transfer them, in their containers, to a dark cupboard, where the temperature may be 65°–70° (18°–21°C). At this time, water them generously, and when the flower buds stand well out, transfer the container to a place with subdued light for a few days. Covering it with newspaper helps to lengthen the flower stem and you should cut off unwanted side shoots and flowering stems. After this, give the bulbs progressively more and more light, and finally put them into their flowering position.

Daffodils. Plant in summer to bloom about five months later. They need to be kept covered in a cool dark place for ten to twelve weeks, and then transferred to a lighter place where there is a temperature of 45°–50°F (7°–10°C) until the flower buds appear. After this you should ideally keep them in a temperature of 50°–55°F (10°–13°C).

Tulips. Varieties such as Brilliant Star Maximus, Christmas Marvel and Marshal Joffre will bloom indoors in mid-winter if they are planted in late summer and kept covered in a cool dark place for three months. After this they should be transferred to a dark place indoors, where there is a temperature of 65°F (18°C). When their shoots have grown two inches, move them to a lighter spot with a steady temperature of 68°F (20°C). If you want them for later flowering, plant in early autumn.

All of the bulbs so far mentioned are those that last indoors for one flowering season only. The most common of the permanent bulbs are:

Amaryllis (Hippeastrum). These bulbs have spectacular pinky-red flowers with long yellow stamens. They are easy to grow indoors and will flourish if you adhere to the following procedure.

Soak the roots and lower part of the bulb in luke-warm water for several days. Put sufficient compost, which should be composed of good loam and leaf-mould, plus a little silver sand, into the growing container to form a cone. Place the bulb with its roots spread out on top of this and cover with fibre to halfway up the bulb.

Put the pot on a warm mantelpiece or radiator shelf – the resulting bottom heat will encourage the bulb's development. When the buds are formed, transfer the pot to a sunny window-sill. Water it sparingly at first, although this can gradually be increased, and use tepid water. Water it always from the top, *never the bottom.*

When the bulb has stopped flowering, put the pot in a cool place. Gradually lessen the frequency of watering as the plant finishes growing, so that you give it almost nothing during the winter. Keep it in a cool, frost-free place in winter and in early spring, top-dress the pot and put it back in a warm place. Water it in the same way as before, increasing the frequency as its growth progresses. From the time the buds appear until foliage growth stops, *Amaryllis* benefit from regular feeds of liquid manure.

Nerine bowdenii is an elegant pot plant, which may be grown from a bulb and is treated throughout in exactly the same way as an amaryllis.

Vallota Speciosa, (Vallota purpurea) is a beautiful permanent bulb plant that is popularly known as the Scarborough Lily. It has heads of trumpet-shaped blooms that are scarlet, but sometimes have other tones of red or white. These appear in late summer, and its elegant foliage lasts throughout the winter.

The Scarborough Lily is easy to grow and thrives in two parts sandy loam and one part leaf-mould. Keep this just damp during autumn and winter and increase watering frequency in spring and summer. It likes a sunny position and you can keep it in the same pot for three or four years. Top-dress it each spring, and then give the plant feeds of liquid manure until flowering time.

Cacti and Succulents

Succulent plants are the 'camels' of the vegetable world, able to store up food and water for use, not on rainy days, but during periods of prolonged drought. Although it has become common practice to talk of Cacti and Succulents as two groups of plants, this is technically incorrect. Cacti Plants, which all belong to one family, and have generally originated in places where they need to be able to exist for long periods without water, are in fact, succulents. They are probably the most popular of all succulent plants, and there are few, if any other groups of plants composed entirely of succulents. This is because other individual plants from various plant genera have developed succulent qualities in order to cope with the living conditions in which they have found themselves. Thus plants, now classified as succulents, are found to be members of at least twenty, widely varied plant families.

Succulent plants have become adapted so that they can reduce the loss of water by evaporation from their tissues and store it instead, either in their leaves or stems or occasionally, in both. This has given rise to two main types of plants – leaf succulents and stem succulents.

Stem succulents usually have no leaves, except sometimes very small ones on young growth, and these soon fall off. Instead the green tissues of the stems take over the normal function of the leaves, such as transpiration and the manufacture of food. The stems themselves are usually very thick and full of water storage tissue, and are mostly, either cylindrical or spherical in shape, sometimes deeply ribbed. These ribs enable the plant to expand or contract as it absorbs or loses water.

Leaf succulents have plump, rounded leaves full of water storage tissue. They are often coated with wax, meal or hairs, all of which help to reduce water loss from the surface. In many cases these succulents have fleshy stems as well, but the leaves play the most important part in food manufacture.

The fact that most succulents tend to be spherical or cylindrical in shape, at least in their water-storing areas, has doubtless evolved because it is the most efficient way of obtaining the maximum volume with the minimum surface area. This means that evaporation from the surface area is minimized.

An unenlightened definition of Cacti might class them all as 'spiny' plants, but this would be quite untrue. Whilst some are strongly armed, others are actually quite spineless. All cacti, however, have areoles, which are small pincushion-like structures scattered over the stems. Offshoots, branches and spines, when present, come from these areoles, and their presence is the way to distinguish a cacti from other stem succulents, which do not have them. In addition all cacti flowers have the same general design, while those of other succulents differ enormously, according to which family they belong.

There are two main categories of cacti popular for growing indoors – Desert Cacti and Epiphytic Cacti. They are both stem succulents, and have either no leaves or only small temporary ones.

Desert Cacti

As their name suggests, Desert Cacti are those that originated in the hot, arid conditions of the desert. The most well-known are probably the spiny, tall or round plants, that we associate with the deserts of America, but many others are found growing on rocky mountain sides and in grassy areas, as well as in the sandy regions of Mexico and South America.

To be grown most successfully indoors, Desert cacti like a growing medium, composed of equal parts of sifted heavy loam, coarse sand and a mixture of four parts finely broken brick and one part old mortar rubble. This will produce a well-drained compost, but since the food content of the soil does not last forever, the plants really need re-potting annually.

A minimum winter temperature of 41°F (5°C) is acceptable to most desert cacti, but they do like lots of sunlight if they are to flourish and flower freely. A south facing window-sill is a good spot. In their natural surroundings they are subject to bouts of heavy rain, in between which, the ground dries out completely. They are therefore not used to having their roots in soil that remains damp for long periods of time. Such conditions are best simulated by watering regularly during spring and summer, and allowing the compost to dry out each time, before watering is repeated.

This alternation of wet and dry spells also helps to encourage flowering.

During the winter, watering should be considerably reduced, but if the cacti are kept in a very dry atmosphere, they will need some water to prevent them shrivelling excessively. One reason for keeping them rather dry at this time is that if they grow in the poor light of winter, they are likely to become distorted and may well rot the following year. Flowering is also affected by the winter's treatment.

Desert cacti are easy to reproduce from cuttings. Some plants form off-sets (miniature 'plants' attached to the parent), which can be removed and allowed to dry for two or three days before they are potted-up in the usual way. This drying period is always allowed for cacti and other succulent cuttings as it prevents rot from spreading into the fleshy stems. Because of their succulent properties, they do not wilt as other cuttings from other plants would.

The 'clustering' desert cacti plants will have rooted 'pups' (off-sets) around the base of the parent, and these you can remove and pot-up immediately. If the plant does not form off-sets, cut off a section of stem and pot it after drying for about a week. Keep the base of the parent plant as it will often sprout again and will subsequently form a number of off-sets around the cut top. The best time to take any cuttings is between April and May.

Epiphytic Cacti

These cacti grow on rocks and in the tropical rain forests of America, among the debris caught up in the branches of trees. They are not parasites, but derive nutriment from decaying vegetable matter.

Epiphytic cacti have flattened, slightly succulent stems, sometimes incorrectly thought to be leaves. These stems may consist of short segments as in the popular 'Christmas Cactus' (see page 74), and flowers are produced on the end of them. Alternatively the stems may be long and strap-like, as in the *epiphyllums* (see page 74), in which case the flowers usually appear from the sides of them.

Epiphytic cacti need a good, porous soil. The potting mixture given for Desert cacti will be satisfactory if it has additional generous proportions of sifted peat and well-rotted cow manure or leaf mould. Soil-less composts are also suitable, but in the case of the *epiphyllums* in particular, the lime-free type of compost is best. (Because of their dislike of lime, it is also better to omit the mortar rubble when potting *epiphyllums*.) Epiphytic cacti need re-potting annually.

As they grow naturally in woodlands, epiphytic cacti need less sun than desert cacti, but being exposed to sunlight for part of the day helps to ensure good blooming. An east-facing window-sill is a good spot as it will capture the early morning sun, but will be in shade during the heat of the day. Water epiphytes freely, particularly in the spring when the buds are forming. When they have finished flowering, don't water them for a month or so

to allow them to rest. After this, resume watering gradually – they will need very little during the winter, particularly if they are kept in a cool place. A guide is to keep them just moist, and never let them dry out completely. They like winter temperatures that generally do not fall below 45°F (7°C).

When in bud epiphytes appreciate feeding once a fortnight or so with a tomato-type fertilizer.

These cacti grow rapidly and when they have outgrown a six-inch pot, they should be re-started. To do this, cut a stem from an *epiphyllum* (see page 74), or a few segments from the *schlumbergeras* and *rhipsalidopsis* (see pages 74). Leave these for a few days to dry out as explained under Desert cacti, and then pot them in the usual way. Cuttings are best taken in April or May, although it is quite possible to take them any time during the spring and summer.

All cacti – whether desert or epiphyte – are able to withstand gas and other obnoxious fumes to some extent. Their tendency to get dusty, particularly if they are knobbly and bristly is best dealt with by stroking with a soft brush. Turn pots regularly so that each part of the plant gets an equal share of light, and grows evenly.

Before discussing some types individually, all that remains to be said is that cacti are generally easy to grow and will resist a considerable amount of neglect, although, as we have shown already, the common belief that 'they never need watering' is a fallacy. However they do make ideal house plants when spare time and experience is somewhat limited.

Unless otherwise stated, care for the following cacti as previously described.

Desert Cacti

Cereus jamacaru. This is an intriguing, angular, and columnar cactus with bluish coloured stems. It rarely flowers indoors, but as it is rather tall, it is an attractive accent plant to grow in a dish arrangement of cacti.

Echinopsis eyriesii. This is a popular Cactus that flourishes under almost any conditions. It is the best known member of the *Echinopsis rhodotricha* cacti, and when young it is almost spherical in shape with a dark, shiny green skin, supporting spines on its ribs. As it becomes an adult, its growth changes to columnar and it can reach a height of three feet. It has lovely white flowers which grow at the top of high stems.

It requires a heavy, rich, soil, slight shade and adequate watering while growing. In the winter it needs occasional watering, fairly good light, and ideally, a temperature of not less than 50°F (10°C).

Echinopsis 'Golden Dream' is a hybrid *Echinopsis* cactus and is a vigorous and hardy plant. It has a globular plant body, growing up to six inches across and divided into ribs with short, brownish spines. Offsets form around the base and may be used for propagation as previously described. It has lovely golden-yellow flowers which appear in summer. They are two to three inches across and are slightly scented.

Chamaecereus silvestrii. Commonly known as the Peanut Cactus, this is a good species for the beginner to grow. It originates from Western Argentina where it grows among grass and low bushes. It has cylinder-shaped, prostrate stems or branches, pale green in colour and dotted with white spines. The stems turn from pale green in winter, to violet in hot sun. They produce small sections or branchlets which are easily removed, and actually frequently drop off naturally. They may be used for propagation.

The stems also produce furry, brown buds which open in May into numerous beautiful erect, bell-shaped vermilion flowers with golden anthers.

This cactus is particularly hardy if kept fairly dry and will survive the winter happily at a temperature of 32°F (0°C) if necessary.

Echinocactus grusonii. This is known as the Barrel or Hedgehog Cactus and comes from the deserts of central Mexico. The young seedlings are round-shaped and have tubercles which carry stout golden spines. As the plant gets bigger, the tubercles merge into ribs. Mature specimens of this cactus can be as much as a yard across, but if they reached this size, they would be very old, as it takes about ten years for a specimen in cultivation to make a diameter of six inches!

Echinocactus grusonii are known to have small yellow flowers, but they are seldom produced indoors, mostly because of the poor light intensity.

Echinocereus blankii. This is often considered to be one of the most colourful of all desert cacti. It is upright when young, but its dark green, long, round branches eventually become prostrate. They have groupings of eight or nine black or white spines and the plant produces abundant violet flowers. It is a hardy plant and will sometimes grow outdoors, but it needs to be in good light.

Other varieties of *Echinocereus* are:

Echinocereus knippelianus which has a dark green, almost globular stem. It is divided by five ribs which carry weak white spines, and pink flowers, which are produced in profusion in May. It is slow-growing.

Echinocereus gelmannii, which is also slow growing, but is appreciated for its thick covering of yellow to red-brown spines.

Echinocereus pectinatus. Also slow-growing, it has a thick stem about three inches in diameter, branching from the base and covered with short white spines, arranged in a comb-like pattern. Its large pink flowers appear in June, and in some specimens, are sweetly scented. In common with most echinocereus, it is hardy in winter if it is kept dry. It also needs particularly good drainage.

Astrophytum myriostigma. It requires little imagination to see how this easy-to-grow cactus acquired its popular name of Bishop's Mitre. Although it is globular

when young, it becomes columnar with age and can grow to a height of two feet. Its green skin is thickly covered with small, grey-white felted spots and it has large yellow flowers, growing usually from its crown. In winter it needs dry, light conditions with temperature of about 50°F (10°C).

Epiphytic Cacti

Zygocactus truncatus. One of the best known and loved of the epiphytic cacti, this is the Christmas Cactus. As may be imagined, it usually begins to bloom towards the end of November, and is often at its best around Christmas-time. It is a pendulous spreading plant with long segmented stems. From the end of these grow its cerise-pink flowers with their many petals, which give the flowers a tassel-like appearance. It needs adequate watering through its winter growing period.

Schlumbergera gaertneri, or *Rhipsalidopsis gaertneri* has the same pendulous, spreading habit of *Zygocactus truncatus.* It produces its scarlet and violet flowers in Spring, often around Easter time, and is known as the Easter Cactus, or Whitsun Cactus. Its leaf-like green stems have purplish, notched edges and not many bristles and the flowers grow from the top joint, often in groups.

It can be grown in a pot, but will also grow happily in a hanging basket or on sphagnum moss, attached to a piece of bark.

Rhipsalidopsis rosea is related to the above, and is also sometimes called the Easter Cactus. It is a small shrub, about nine inches high and again consists of dozens of stem segments about one inch long, with short bristles at the ends. The stems vary from green to dark red, and the pale-pink, bell-shaped flowers cover the plant during May. When it stops flowering, it looks quite shrivelled, but after a few weeks, it comes back into growth again.

Aporacactus flagelliformis. This epiphyte has long, glossy, green, narrow stems which later turn grey. They somewhat resemble rat's tails, hence the plant's popular name – Rat Tail Cactus. It has lovely, colourful, profuse flowers that emerge from these stems, usually at the beginning of spring.

There are a number of hybrids of this species that produce flowers in abundance in a range of colours. A particularly lovely one is *Aporacactus flagelliformis* 'Vulkan' which has scarlet flowers.

Epiphyllums. This group of cacti have received a lot of attention from horticulturists and there are a great number of beautiful flowering hybrids on the market, in all colours except blue. Many of these are also pleasantly scented. Together with the *rhipsalidopsis* and *schlumbergeras,* already mentioned, hybrid epiphyllums are among the most popular epiphytic cacti to be grown indoors.

Epiphyllum ackermannii is a delightful epiphytic cactus that has an appropriate and descriptive popular name – the Orchid Cactus. It has flattened, dark stems with a few spines, from which emerge its gorgeous, large, deep-crimson flowers.

Notable hybrids of this species are 'Cooperil', which has large, white scented flowers; 'London Glory', which has orange-red and magenta flowers; 'London Surprise' which has large orange flowers; 'Exotique' which has purplish flowers, and 'Sunburst' which has orange flowers.

Opuntia microdasys. One of the most intriguing cacti to be grown indoors. It is popularly known as Prickly Pear or Bunny's Ears, both of which are descriptive of its appearance. It has flat stem segments up to about six inches long and emerald green in colour. They are dotted with little collections of fine barbed hairs, which may be white, yellow or dark reddish-brown, depending on the variety. This cactus which is extremely tolerant is grown for its form and it rarely flowers as a pot plant. If given a free root run in a greenhouse bed, however, it produces yellow flowers in May.

Opuntia basilaris. Related to the above, this cactus has pads about eight inches long of a beautiful bluish colour, dotted with a collection of dark-brown, fine, barbed hairs. Branches form from the base, producing a large clump. Again, although it rarely blooms as a pot plant, it is able to produce red flowers.

Mammillaria bocasana. Often known as the Pincushion Cactus, this cactus belongs to a large group of cacti. It is a small rounded plant and produces blue to green, short side-shoots which are completely covered with fine white spines, giving the whole mass a bluish-grey colour. The yellowish flowers, which have a central reddish stripe on the outer petals appear through this covering.

Other notable *Mammillaria* varieties are: *Mammillaria wildii*, which is among the hardiest of the species and has soft flesh, yellow, hooked spines and whitish flowers that grow in a ring at the top; and *Mammillaria prolifera*, which clusters freely, forming a cushion of small heads all covered with fine white spines. It has creamy flowers which appear in late spring and are often followed by orange-red berries. The heads can be knocked off very easily, so handle this plant carefully.

All mammillaria are easy to grow, resisting adverse conditions even to the extent of withstanding erroneous treatment and neglect. A good plant for beginners!

Gymnocalycium bruchii. This is a miniature cactus from Argentina which eventually clusters from the base. Its globular plant body is divided by twelve ribs which are covered in neat white spines. In May, its pink flowers open. These are over one inch long, and since the plant may be less than one inch across, it often is hidden by flowers.

Other species of *Gymnocalycium* are: *Gymnocalycium quehlianum*, which is the shape of a flattened sphere and has ribs composed of knobs, with brownish spines radiating from them. Its skin is dull grey-green and turns brownish in the sun. Whitish funnel-shaped flowers with a carmine centre grow from the crown.

Gymnocalysium baldianum. This forms a plant body about three inches across and has nine ribs bearing yellowish spines.

The flowers, produced in May are usually deep red, but occasionally specimens are found with intense pink flowers.

Gymnocalycium platense. This is a globular plant which eventually grows to be three or more inches in diameter. The plant body is greyish-green and is divided into twelve or fourteen ribs. These carry short whitish spines, and the plant produces lots of white flowers in the early summer.

Rebutia marsoneri. This is a small cactus which eventually grows approximately two inches high and three inches across. Its body is flattened spherical in shape and is pale green, although it becomes grey as it ages. It is covered in spines that vary in colour from white to deep yellow. It has intensely red buds that break into beautiful golden-yellow flowers.

Other species are:

Rebutia pseudodeminuta, which has a flattened sphere no more than two and a half inches in diameter. It flowers abundantly with red and golden flowers.

Rebutia calliantha 'Krainziana', which has globular stems that are dark green and covered with short white spines. It has large, orange flowers that appear in rings around the base of the plant in May.

Rebutia miniscula 'Violaciflora', which is a small clustering plant that flowers when it is only about one inch across. It is light green with short ginger spines and it produces its magenta-pink flowers from its base in April and May. It is self-fertile, and if left undisturbed will eventually be surrounded by dozens of little self-sown seedlings.

Succulents

As mentioned earlier, other succulent plants belong to a wide variety of plant families. Cultivation of most of these, however, is very similar to that of desert cacti. In general they need plenty of water in summer and sufficient to keep them just slightly moist in winter. They like some grit or sharp sand in their growing medium and they will flourish best if kept in a very sunny place. A winter temperature of 41°F (5°C) is adequate for most succulents.

Like cacti, they are comparatively easy to raise from seed, providing you use a good seed compost or a soil-less one. This should be thoroughly moistened and the seeds scattered on the surface. A plastic bag secured over the container will help to conserve a moist atmosphere, and a temperature of 70°–80°F (21°–27°C) is needed for germination.

Euphorbia splendens. Otherwise known as the Crown of Thorns, this is an attractive succulent member of the same plant family as the Poinsettia (see page 55). It is a shrubby plant, with bright, scarlet bracts produced in pairs, and surrounding tiny yellow flowers. It is characterized by its long, sharp thorns, which can be most damaging to the hands, if it is carelessly handled.

It likes a winter temperature of about 45°F (7°C), during which time it needs little watering. It is a deciduous plant, but a relative – *Euphorbia bojeri* – is an evergreen and produces flowers throughout most of the year.

Gasteria maculata has long tongue-shaped leaves arranged in two rows. These are dark green with white markings. It also has reddish flowers carried on a slender stem.

Gasteria maculata produces off-sets freely, which can be left to form a plant group, or potted-up individually.

Stapelia variegata. A curious and strangely beautiful plant that has smooth, long branching leaves that are light green and mottled, with teeth-like prominences. Its bizarre flowers are star-shaped, with five petals, yellowish in colour and covered with brown speckles and stripes. They are produced continuously during summer and late autumn. The plant also has large, horn-shaped seed pods.

Kalanchoe blossfeldiana is one of a very large species. It is known for its panicles of scarlet flowers that grow on slender, tall stems during the winter. It is a shrubby plant with dark-green, red-edged succulent leaves. During its winter growing season it must be kept well watered.

Of the same family and suitable for growing in pots are *Kalanchoe kewensis* and *Kalanchoe tomentosa*.

Aeonium domesticum. The aeoniums are native to the Canary Islands, although beautiful specimens may be found growing naturally in the gardens of Cornwall. *Aeonium domesticum* has almost circular leaves covered with fine hairs, and during the summer it produces yellow flowers. These plants are often grown in rock gardens during the summer.

Aloe variegata is a native plant of Cape Province, South Africa. Its popular names include Partridge-breasted Aloe, Falcon Feather and Tiger Aloe. It is mainly attractive for its stemless rosette of triangular shaped, grey-green leaves which have whitish spots. It is a robust plant and grows easily to an eventual height of twelve inches or so. It produces many off-sets which are attached to the parent plant by underground stems and has small orange, bell-shaped flowers that grow on a stout stem in March.

Aloe jucunda, of the same family is a miniature aloe, native to Somalia. It has small flat rosettes, which are about four inches across and the bright green leaves have small teeth along their edges with the characteristic white spots found in many aloes. Its flowers are pink, and open in springtime. *Aloe jucunda* clusters freely, and the individual heads can be used to start new plants.

Other aloes recommended for pot culture are *Aloe arborescens*, *Aloe brevifolia* and *Aloe humilia*.

Ceropegia woodii, known as Heart's Entangled, is a trailing succulent plant grown mainly for its foliage. It has heart shaped leaves, which grow in pairs along its long, reddish-brown stems. The upper surfaces of the leaves are dark green with a heavy grey mottle, making them appear silvery. *Crassula arborescens* is a tallish plant, which makes a good accent in a dish garden. It has greyish-green leaves with red dots.

Belonging to the same family are:

Crassula falcata, which is popular for its

striking red flowers and bluish-grey leaves; and *Crassula teres*, which is a miniature plant with broad leaves that are closely packed around the stem to form a short column. It has tiny white flowers that are stemless, and as the plant ages, it clusters to form attractive groups. It likes to be grown in a very open compost, kept in a sunny position and not over-watered.

Echeveria glauca or *Echeveria secunda glauca* has beautiful glaucous rosettes of blue-green, red-margined leaves, from which rise bright red and yellow flowers on arching stems.

Another member of the family that can be grown successfully indoors is *Echeveria derenbergii*, which is a dwarf plant and forms an almost stemless rosette about three inches across, which is soon surrounded by numerous off-sets. It has plump, pale green leaves which have a white, waxy coating. Its reddish-yellow flowers open in the spring.

Cotyledon undulata. This succulent plant has attractive large leaves, narrow at the base and fanning out, with a wavy edge. They are covered with white powdery bloom, which gives them a greyish appearance. Never water them from above, or the powdery bloom will be washed off. The flowers of *Cotyledon undulata* are cream with red stripes and bell-shaped.

Sedum adolphii is a low semi-shrub, with fleshy or semi-woody branches. Its leaves are about one and a half inches long, fleshy, pale green in colour and oval-shaped. They grow at the end of each of the branches, forming a close, rather charming cluster.

Other species that make good house plants are *Sedum allantoides*, which has whitish-green, stout, keel-shaped leaves, and *Sedum pachyphyllum*, which has similarly shaped leaves that are green, tipped with red.

The two succulent plants discussed below belong to the South African mesembryanthemum family and grow naturally among stones, which they closely resemble. They are commonly referred to as 'Pebble Plants'.

Conophytum pearsonii is easy-to-grow and forms unusual clumps of rounded stems, which are broadly conical with a flattened crown. The stems are shaped like small apples and are smooth and bluish-green in colour. Pale violet flowers appear during September and October, which is the beginning of the plant's growing season.

During its summer resting period, a new body forms inside the old stem, absorbing all the substances from it. Eventually all that remains is the skin, which dries and protects the new plant from the heat of the sun and excessive water evaporation. At this time, the plant looks like a stone, and is known as a 'living pebble'.

Lithops bella. Before this plant blooms, it consists of two fleshy, plump leaves, which are about one inch high, and resemble a roundish pebble with a fissure across its flattened top. In the autumn a daisy like white flower grows from this fissure. The new leaves grow inside the old ones exactly as in *Conophytum pearsonii*.

Plants from Pips

Growing indoor 'fruit trees' from fruit stones and pips is something most 'indoor gardeners' have tried at sometime in their lives, even if only when they were children. It can be an equally interesting and rewarding hobby or pursuit for an adult, however, and it is remarkable how easily many of the fruit pips and stones discarded from our meal table will root themselves if treated correctly. Given time they will become most attractive house plants.

The pips of the more common of the citrus fruits – oranges, lemons, tangerines and grapefruit – can all be planted at any time of the year and will eventually grow into small trees. When selecting these pips to plant, choose really plump ones, which will be found in fruits throughout the year. When you have decided which ones to use, wash them thoroughly and soak them in cold water for a full day. Fill an average size flower pot with damp commercial potting compost, and plant three pips around the pot, so that they are half- to one-inch below the surface of the compost.

Cover the pips, either by placing a large glass jam jar over the pot or by covering it with a polythene bag, supported on four stakes pushed into the soil, and tied firmly just below the brim. This will serve to give a sealed, humid atmosphere.

Alternatively you could plant the pips in one of the more recently introduced special 'propagating pots' which have a well-fitting, transparent, plastic hood. Once planted, put the pips in a warm, dark place until they have germinated. Transfer them to a light

place, and remove the transparent covering after a few days. As soon as a pair of leaves appear, transplant each tiny plant into its own six-inch pot, using a commercial potting compost again. Keep them in a light place with reasonable warmth from then on, and they should develop into attractive little trees with very decorative, glossy, dark-green foliage.

Other favourites for indoor cultivation are the stones of apricots, avocado pears, dates, lychees and peaches. These will all produce very charming indoor plants, but they are harder to persuade to root than the pips of citrus fruits. In general the initial procedure for raising plants from these stones is the same as that described for pips. It is as well, however to plant a few spare date stones, because many of these appear to be infertile. You will also have to be very patient and keep all the stones in a dark place for much longer than citrus pips before they begin to germinate. Date stones will take at least two months before they show signs of germinating, and it could be as long as four months before avocado pears show any hopeful signs.

In all cases, allow a few weeks to pass after germination before re-potting the seedlings, this time into three-inch pots. Use a commercial potting compost as the growing medium.

These plants need to be kept warm and well watered if they are to flourish. Re-pot them as necessary. And as a word of warning, remember that the avocado pear in its natural habitat, grows into a sixty foot high tree, so it can become rather too tall to be accommodated in the normal house!

Pineapple plants are fun to grow indoors and their silvery, long-toothed, curving foliage make them very beautiful, yet inexpensive, houseplants. If pineapples are grown in a warm room, they will often bear fruit only two years after planting.

When preparing a pineapple to eat, cut off the fleshy top with a rosette of healthy leaves (this should be done in the spring). Remove the lower leaves to uncover about one inch of the bare stump. Leave this to dry out for a few days, then plant it in moist sand, and tie it to a stake to support it. Put it in a warm place and water the sand as it dries out. Probe about at the base of the pineapple about once a fortnight to see if the roots are growing. As soon as they appear, transfer the pineapple to a small pot filled with commercial potting compost.

During the summer, keep the pineapple plant in a warm place and water it fairly frequently. Transplant it as soon as it becomes pot-bound. During the winter, keep it in a warm place again, but reduce the watering considerably. Re-pot it the following spring and begin to increase the rate of watering again. When the pineapple begins to grow a fruit stem, feed it regularly with liquid feed.

Indoor Gardens

An attractive and effective way of using indoor plants to make a focal point or display is to group a selection together in a dish or bottle garden.

Dish gardens are easily started and maintained, but you must bear in mind that the choice of plants is of paramount importance. They must all like the same growing conditions, in terms of temperature, watering, light and so on. In order to be aesthetically pleasing the arrangement should be composed of plants varying in height, foliage, shapes and colours. A well-proportioned grouping, generally speaking, should always contain one predominantly tall plant with a few bushy ones of varying lower heights to act as foils, and one or two trailers to overhang and soften the sides of the dish. In addition, the plants should be more or less equally vigorous, so that none overruns its neighbours.

There are all sorts of containers that are suitable for dish gardens, and you should train yourself to see potential in unusual things. Keep a look-out in junk shops for odd soup tureens, an old washstand basin perhaps, or maybe a preserving pan. Modern shops offer some possibilities too – wooden troughs, clay dishes, and basketwork and wrought iron troughs which have metal linings – all make attractive containers for an indoor garden.

There are two approaches to planting out a dish garden, the first of which applies if you are using plants that all like much the same soil conditions. Fill the dish with a layer of stones and crocks to ensure it has

(below) A carboy bottle
garden
(right) An attractive
stand display of indoor
plants

adequate drainage. Put a layer of compost (to suit your plants) on top. Gently tap the plants you have selected out of their individual pots and plant them in the container in the usual way. Remember to keep your indoor garden in a spot which complies with the growing requirements of the plants you have put in it. Feeding and watering will be similarly tempered.

For the alternative method you will need a fairly deep container (a trough type would be particularly suitable). Fill the bottom with a layer of moist peat and then stand the plants you have selected on top, *still in their individual pots*. Pack the container with more damp peat, until this is level with the rim of the pots.

The advantages of this sort of container garden are obvious – plants that like different soils, although not environmental conditions, can be mixed together, and also as each plant can be watered individually you can also mix plants with different watering requirements. Flowering pot plants and bulbs can be included in the arrangement at the relevant times of year to add a splash of colour and plant pots can be positioned at varying angles to enhance the arrangement. If the rims of the pots are visible and are spoiling the display, disguise them with stones, driftwood or moss.

Another way of adding interest to a dish garden is to sink a florist's metallic or glass tube into the compost in the dish. This can be filled with cut flowers to give freshness and colour.

There are many combinations of plants that will make charming, successful dish gardens, and half the fun involved is in making your own choice. In order to give you some guidance should you want it, a few typical groupings are:

Large Size Arrangements
1. *Chamaedorea elegans* 'Bella', *Dracaena sanderi*, *Dracaena sanderi* 'Borenquensis', *Hedera helix* 'Scutifolia', *Peperomia obtusifolia* 'Variegata', *Sansevieria trifasciata* 'Hahnii', *Scindapsus aurea*, *Syngonium podophyllum*.
2. *Aphelandra squarrosa*, *Dracaena sanderi*, *Ficus benjamina*, *Fittonia verschaffeltii*, *Hedera canariensis* 'Variegata', *Peperomia argyreia*, *Peperomia hederifolia*.

Medium Size Arrangements
1. *Asplenium nidus avis*, *Dracaena deremensis* 'Warnecki', *Grevillea robusta*, *Peperomia caperata*, Poinsettia.
2. *Calathea ornata*, *Ficus elastica* 'Decora', *Hedera helix* 'Glacier', *Neoregelia carolinae* 'Tricolor'.

Small Size Arrangements
1. *Hedera helix* 'Chicago' and Saintpaulia.
2. *Chlorophytum capense* 'Variegatum', *Begonia rex* and *Peperomia rotundifolia*.

The two last arrangements are quite suitable for a pedestal vase.

Plants that make extremely attractive and easy-to-maintain dish gardens are cacti, but owing to their unique soil requirements and growing conditions, they should not be mixed with other indoor plants, except perhaps some succulents which have similar requirements. The large number of cacti varieties, however, makes it quite possible to plant out dish gardens using different species of cacti only.

Miniature gardens are also a great 'indoor tradition' with house plant enthusiasts. They are initially rather more complicated than dish gardens as they should include small garden features, such as tiny paths, ponds (made from mirrors), bridges, lawns (made from moss), little tree-type plants and so on. This means that they need careful designing in the initial stage, but the planting and maintenance procedures are the same as for dish gardens, and the same rules for plant selection apply.

Gardens grown in bottles have also become increasingly popular and understandably so, as they make an attractive asset to any room. They are completely self contained, clean and neat and will provide interest and amusement for years.

Bottle gardens are usually constructed in large glass carboys, which can be quite expensive to acquire. Any type of clear glass container can be used, providing it has a large enough neck to allow the plants to be inserted. (It must be clear glass so that the plants inside will get the maximum light.) Another type of vessel that can be similarly planted out is a glass terrarium, which usually consists of a ten- or twelve-inch diameter bowl fitted with an air-tight lid. Quite a satisfactory terrarium can be improvised, using an old battery jar or a goldfish bowl. In addition old sweet and pickle jars are ideal for bottle gardens.

The advantage of growing plants in these glass containers is that a very moist, warm, draught-free atmosphere is produced and maintained constantly. Thus delicate plants requiring such conditions can be successfully grown at home, without any discomfort to you and your family. The skill in a bottle garden lies in the preparation and planting, particularly if you are using a carboy which is obviously more difficult to plant out than a wide-mouthed terrarium. Considerable dexterity and patience is needed to plant out a carboy successfully, but the results are so attractive and easy to maintain that it is quite worth the effort.

The following instructions apply mainly to planting out a carboy, but the same principles apply to other types of bottles, terrarium and goldfish bowls.

First you must make some gardening 'tools', such as a 'trowel' and 'fork-cum-rake', to facilitate planting. You will need some two-foot long bamboo canes which will act as handles to the various implements. To make a 'trowel', cut off and slightly straighten the handle of an old teaspoon. Stick it into the hollow centre of one of the bamboo canes, using a plastic padding adhesive to hold it in place if necessary. Alternatively, bind the spoon to the cane using stiff wire. To make a 'fork-cum-rake', follow the same procedure using an old table fork instead of a teaspoon.

Another useful tool is a 'soil rammer' which you can make from an old cotton reel. Smear the end of a bamboo cane with adhesive and then push this into the centre of the cotton reel.

For the maintenance of your bottle garden you will also need some sort of pruning implement, and a pair of tongs to remove cuttings and dead leaves. To make a long-handled pruning knife, split the end of a two-foot long bamboo cane and fix a razor blade securely into the split. The long handled tongs you can make by shortening a pair of light kitchen tongs and giving them long bamboo handles in the same way as you did the trowel and fork. If you do not have such a pair of tongs, or they are too big to go through the top of the bottle, you can do the same job using two long sticks manipulated within the bottle, like chopsticks. This may require a little practice to perfect!

To prepare the bottle, first wash it very thoroughly. This is particularly important if you are using a carboy, since they are often used to carry strong acid. Use lots of detergent and water, and finish by rinsing very thoroughly. Leave the bottle to dry out completely inside, (you can speed this process by blowing round the interior with a hair drier!). Do not attempt to begin filling the carboy while it is still wet as the soil will just stick to the sides and smear the glass.

When the carboy is quite dry, line the bottom of it with a substantial layer of stones or crocks, preferably mixed with crushed charcoal – this is important as there is obviously no means of free drainage. Then pour a quantity of moist commercial potting compost on top. You will find that if you insert a cylinder of paper or cardboard into the neck of the carboy, and pour the compost through this, you will lessen the likelihood of badly spattering the sides of the carboy with soil. Two to three inches of compost is the absolute minimum depth needed for planting, but in larger containers, four to six inches is really preferable.

When you have sufficient compost in the bottom, use the fork to make a few small hills and 'undulations' which will help to increase the quality of the display. Then lightly consolidate the soil by using the cotton reel rammer.

Gather together the plants you have decided to use, and try out a few arrangements of them in a bowl of compost the same circumference size as the bottle interior, to find the most attractive display. It is really essential to do this, because manipulation inside the carboy is both difficult and limited.

When you are satisfied with the arrangement, make a small hole in the compost with the trowel, and drop in the first plant. Use the tongs or 'chopsticks' to manoeuvre it into position, spread out its roots around its stem as much as possible with the fork and then cover them with soil. Firm up the soil round the roots using the cotton reel rammer. Plant all the remaining plants in their allotted positions in the same way.

It is best to begin planting on the outside of the area and work towards the centre. Make sure that the plants are not squashed too much together, or against the sides of the carboy, although there is no harm in a few leaves touching the glass. You can increase the interest and heighten the display by covering some of the soil with small stones or pieces of moss. In any event, it is essential to firm the compost, so that no gaps remain between it and the roots.

When you have completed the planting, 'wash' the inside of the carboy. The easiest and most efficient way to do this is to wrap a long length of wire round the middle of a small sponge mop, moisten the sponge and wipe it round the insides of the carboy. Water the plants immediately after planting using a small cylindrical garden spray, the nozzle of which should be set at an angle so that it can be inserted inside the carboy. You can also use this to wash off any soil that has stuck to the leaves of the plants.

Finally, close up the top of the carboy and leave it alone. Initially the sides will steam up with condensation, obscuring the contents, but this soon clears. After about two months, open the bottle garden and water it. Close it up again, and thereafter, once a good moisture balance has been established, it should only need watering every eight months to a year. Watch it carefully in the early stages, however, to make sure it does not dry out.

Bottle gardens, ideally like fairly light places, out of direct sunlight which would probably scorch the plants. They like a winter temperature that doesn't fall much below 50°F (10°C). Remember to prune the plants as soon as they get too large or straggly and remove discoloured or dying leaves as you notice them.

Throughout this book, we have mentioned plants that are suitable for bottle gardens. As well as bearing in mind the conditions that prevail in bottle gardens, and choosing plants accordingly, it is advisable to avoid strong-growing plants, which will merely swamp the others. Plants listed below are all suitable:
Acorus gramineus, 'Variegatus', *Adiantum cuneatum, Begonia rex, Chlorophytum capense* 'Variegatum', *Cocos weddelliana, Codiaeum variegatum* Pictum, *Codiaeum pictum* 'Apple Leaf', Cryptanthus, *Ctenanthes oppenheimiana* 'Tricolor', *Cyrtomium falcatum, Dracaena godseffiana, Dracaena sanderi, Ficus pumila, Fittonia verschaffeltii, Helxine soleriolii, Hoya carnosa* 'Variegata', Ivies, *Maranta leuconeura* 'Kerchoveana', *Nephrolepis exalta, Peperomia magnoliifolia, Pilea cadierei* 'Minima', Saintpaulias, *Sansevieria trifasciata* 'Laurentii', and *Saxifraga sarmentosa*.

Plants for Purposes

We mentioned very briefly at the beginning of this book, that thought should be given to the purpose for which the indoor house plant is required, when making a choice. As you will now appreciate, the many varieties in shape, colour and living conditions that prevail in indoor plants makes it possible to find something for every indoor situation. Indeed they can often offer satisfactory and attractive solutions to many domestic situation problems.

In open plan houses, plants can be used to make effective room dividers, and screens. A practical way of making a light screen to divide the drawing and dining areas of a large room is to grow and train *Ficus pumila*, for example, or any of the ivies, up supporting sticks. This could equally as well serve as a screen to conceal the remnants of a meal after a dinner party. A denser divider may be needed in a bed-sitter, perhaps, to act as a barrier between the living section, sleeping quarters or kitchen area. In such a case, *Cissus antarctica*, *Philodendron scandens* or *Tetrastigma voinieriana* would all be suitable plants to use. Climbing house plants also have great aesthetic value when used to frame a large window.

Indoor plants can do much to compensate those who live in a flat or house in a town, and may be deprived of the great joy of a view of their own garden. Two or three house plants, of varying heights, grown on a window sill will produce a delightfully fresh effect, while the more ambitious indoor gardener might perhaps replace the

window sill with a full-length trough in which he plants out an 'indoor garden', (see page 86). Remember in this case however, to install a venetian blind over the window to protect the plants from both sun and frost.

Use house plants, also to hide an empty fireplace during the summer, or all the year round in houses where central heating has been installed, and old fireplaces covered over. Make sure in such cases, however, that the chimney is properly blocked up, or the cold draughts that come howling down, will certainly damage, if not kill, plants. Remember too that plants situated in spots away from the window are in a 'dark place', so either use those plants that require less light, or better still, make the display even more effective by illuminating it with a spotlight.

Indoor plants can play an important role as part of the whole interior design of a room or house. An unembellished light-coloured wall, can be much softened by a single dramatic specimen such as *Ficus elastica* 'Decora' placed in front of it. Or bring relief to such a wall, by training climbing plants in front of it, or by fixing containers or brackets high up on its surface to hold pots of lovely trailing plants. High ceilings can be optically lowered by the presence of an imposing spreading plant, such as *Philodendron selloum*, and use an arrangement of colourful plants, lit with fluorescent bulbs to turn a dark corner into a bright focal point.

We have already mentioned dish and bottle gardens in the preceding chapter. They all have great aesthetic value and can be a valuable asset in providing an interesting display in a living room. Bottle gardens are particularly effective if converted into a table or floor lamp and it is a sure way of making certain the plants are well lit! Remember when you make the lamp to use a fitment that can be easily removed to allow you access to the plants for care and maintenance. An attractive place for a bottle garden lamp is at the head of a staircase, were their fascinating details can be observed by everybody as they go up stairs.

The specimen house plant, growing in its own individual pot, in which it can be seen at its very best, is perhaps the best display of all. Always choose a container that in no way detracts from the beauty of the plant itself. It is amazing how often a plant is shown off to its best advantage when contained in just a simple clay pot.

Thus it can be seen that indoor plants can do much to enliven and bring great charm to a room. Use flowering pot plants to accompany others, to give brightness and colour through the dreary winter months, and use all sorts of plants to bring verdant freshness into the house during summer. Use them to complement your furnishings – plants with large, shiny, rich green leaves will help to lessen the fussiness of a small fabric design, while the small-leaved and variegated foliage of other plants can relieve the starkness of plain materials.

On no account, however, should the use of houseplants be overdone. Keep them under control and use them to highlight a situation not to dominate it or to become the main feature itself.

Plants are becoming increasingly popular in offices too, where they do much to make the office a pleasanter place in which to work. Once again, they can be used to soften the decor of modern offices and to mask the somewhat harsh lines of contemporary office furniture. Climbing plants can be used to form relatively low divisions in open plan offices or to make screens for masking temporary piles of incoming goods or banks of filing cabinets. There is almost an argument that their presence is an aid to tidiness!

It has been claimed that growing plants in offices produces a good psychological effect on the office staff. Certainly the gardeners amongst them will appreciate fresh foliage, and it has long been recognised that green is a restful colour. In towns and cities, plants provide a pleasing contrast to the starkness and shabbiness of the brick buildings which so often form the main view from the window.

The greatest problem of growing plants in offices, however, is their upkeep. How are they to be cared for during hot (or cold) weekends, and holiday periods when the self-appointed, dedicated office plant lover is away? Whilst it is undoubtedly true that even with these unfavourable odds, many plants grown in offices do survive, if not flourish, the more satisfactory answer is for the management to engage a house plant contractor. He will be a specialist able to advise on the most suitable plants and sites for the conditions and purposes. Contractors of this nature work in a variety of ways, some owning and hiring out various plants, and others merely advising on suitable plants for the office concern to buy, which the contractor then maintains.

The problem of finding the right plant for any particular office situation is undoubtedly a tricky one. If you consider the conditions most offices have to offer plants – insufficient light or baking sun, excessive heat, hot radiators, dry air, draughts, tobacco smoke, neglect or over-caring, and deposits of unwanted vending machine drinks – it is certainly a decision best left to the experts! If your office is unprepared to use the contractors' services, the best thing you can do is to assess the conditions that prevail in your office to the best of your ability, and choose house plants that are recommended as being exceptionally tough and hardy!

Index

Acknowledgments

Bernard Alfieri (Natural History Photograph
Agency): p24–5, 69; A-Z Botanical Collection:
p48; Camera Press: p89; W. F. Davidson: p10, 29;
Samuel Dobie & Sons Ltd., Llangollen: p61,
64–5; J. E. Downward: p17; Gover Grey Photo-
graphy: p2, 37; P. Hinous (Connaissance des
Arts): p93; Peter Hunt: p20; Anthony Huxley:
p21; G. E. Hyde: p81; E. A. Over: p77; Jackson &
Perkins: p7, 15, 33, 72–3, 85; Kenneth Scowan:
p53; Harry Smith: p41, 44, 45, 49, 84, 88; Spectrum
Colour Library: p6, 40